"The Stone Lion"
and Other
Chinese
Detective Stories

The authors gratefully acknowledge the assistance of the Salmon Fund of Vassar College during the preparation of the manuscript for this book.

"The Stone Lion" and Other Chinese Detective Stories

The Wisdom of Lord Bau

Yin-lien C. Chin
Yetta S. Center
Mildred Ross

Illustrations by Lu Wang

An East Gate Book

M.E. Sharpe

Armonk, New York ■ London, England

An East Gate Book

Copyright © 1992 by M. E. Sharpe, Inc.

Available in the United Kingdom and Europe from M. E. Sharpe,
Publishers, 3 Henrietta Street, London WC2E 8LU.

Library of Congress Cataloging-in-Publication Data

Lung t'u kung an. English. Selections.
"The Stone lion" and other Chinese detective stories:
the wisdom of Lord Bau /
Yin-lien C. Chin, Yetta S. Center, Mildred Ross.
p.   cm.
"An East gate book."
Translation of: Lung t'u kung an.
Summary: Presents ten tales featuring Lord Ba, a wise judge who was a champion of righ-
teousness and protector of the weak against the powerful.
ISBN 0-87332-634-2 (cloth)
—ISBN 0-87332-635-0 (paper)
[1. Conduct of life—Fiction.
2. Pao, Cheng, 999–1062—Fiction.
3. China—Fiction.]
I. Chin, Yin-lien C.
II. Center, Yetta S.
III. Ross, Mildred.
IV. Title
PZ7.L979116St   1992
[Fic]—dc20
91-46520
CIP
AC

Printed in the United States of America

The paper used in this publication meets the minimum requirements of
American National Standard for Information Sciences—
Permanence of Paper for Printed Library Materials,
ANSI Z39.48–1984.

BM (c) 10   9   8   7   6   5   4   3   2   1
BM (p) 10   9   8   7   6   5   4   3   2   1

For
Alfred, Bonnie, Daniel,
Hsiao-lien, Isabel,
Jacqueline, Stephen

Contents

Introduction   ix

Millstone Street   3

The True Mother   19

A Stolen Stallion   37

The Stone Lion   53

Snow White Goose   71

Palace Plot   87

The Black Bowl   103

Borrowed Clothes   115

A Bloody Handprint   133

Singsong Girl   149

Introduction

With a little stretching of the imagination it might be proposed that some Chinese tales dating from the Sung Dynasty were the precursors of modern detective fiction. Numerous stories in which Lord Bau is the chief protagonist bolster this conjecture. Solver of crimes, righter of wrongs, protector of the weak against the powerful, he has been memorialized for the past thousand years in Chinese literature. He appears also as the central character in hundreds of plays and operas. Over the centuries inventive spinners of yarns have turned him into a folk hero, even elevating him to mythical stature, one possessed of the power to communicate with the dead.

The real Bau Jeng was born in the year 999 in Hefei County, Anhui Province. His life span of sixty-nine years coincided roughly with the reigns of Emperors Jen Dzung (998–1022) and Ren Dzung (1023–1063) of the Northern Sung Dynasty.

About his ancestry almost nothing is known. It is believed that he came from a humble family. If he had a wife and children, little creditable information as to their identity survives. He did sit for the civil service examinations and earned exceptionally high grades. This is attested to by existing records of appointments to a variety of government posts. But this lack of documentation did not hinder the creative output of anecdotes about Lord Bau's personal life.

One that is a favorite among storytellers relates that just prior to Lord Bau's birth his father was frightened by a disquieting nightmare. In his dream he was visited by a hideous monster. According to widely held superstitions of the time, a dream such as this was prophetic. It was a warning that the newborn babe would be an incarnation of the repulsive apparition, a harbinger of bad luck. To rid his family of danger, Lord Bau's father arranged to have his tiny son abandoned on a mountain ledge frequented by tigers. The helpless infant was rescued in the nick of time by an older brother.

A second anecdote also deals with Lord Bau's miraculous escape from the clutches of death. It is said to have taken place when he was a young boy of seven or eight. A jealous sister-in-law prepared a dish of his favorite pancakes, combining a dose of poison with the other ingredients. Just as the unsuspecting youngster was about to take his first bite, his faithful dog jumped up and knocked it out of his hand. The dog devoured the pancake and an hour later was found dead.

In keeping with the Chinese belief in predestination, Lord Bau's dramatic rescues were inevitable. Ordained for greatness, nothing could prevent him from fulfilling his destiny.

In the telling and retelling of events of his real life, and in the stories highlighting his great wisdom as a judge, the elements of fact and fancy have been intertwined in an inseparable web. What does it matter that the truth cannot be neatly divided from the myth? More important is that his name remains synonymous with intelligence, compassion, and, above all else, incorruptibility. This last attribute has endeared him to the Chinese people through the ages. Having grown accustomed to expect only dishonesty and deceit from officials, it is no wonder they clasped the righteous Lord Bau to their breasts.

In this collection of stories translated from Chinese anthologies and retold for the pleasure of English-speaking readers, Lord Bau is cast in the role of wise judge. Across the span of ten centuries his name has been spoken with reverence and remains to this day the symbol of the ideal public official.

"The Stone Lion"
and Other
Chinese
Detective Stories

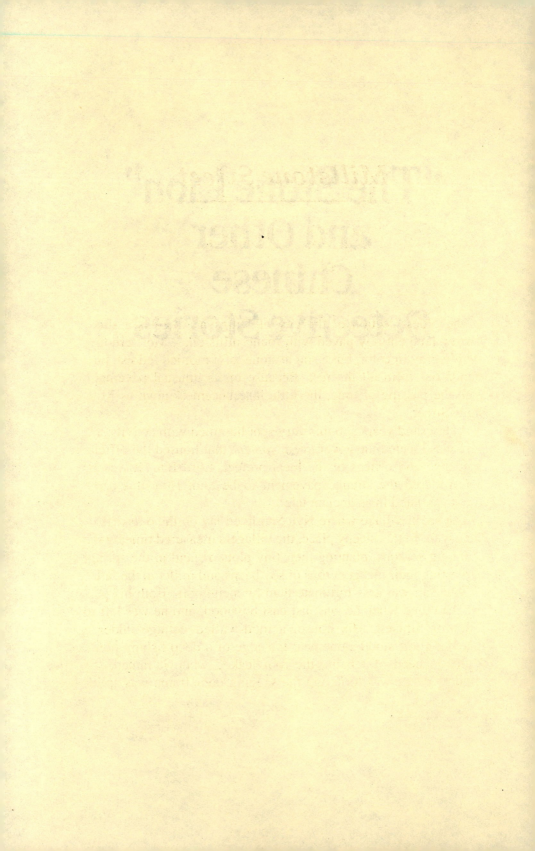

Millstone Street

In the oldest section of the city of Dingsyan there is a short, narrow lane entirely paved with round millstones. Most are uniformly gray in color, but a single stone, of a mottled reddish hue, stands out from all the rest. Because of its unusual pavement, with the passing of time, the little lane became known as Millstone Street.

A thousand years ago this very spot hummed with activity, for here was located the government *yamen** that housed the official residence and offices of the local prefect, Lord Bau. It was he who ordered the strange pavement to be laid. How this came about is related in an ancient tale.

The small village where Nyu San lived lay on the outskirts of Dingsyan. In this sleepy place, the villagers measured time by the changing seasons, planting their tiny plots of land in the spring, harvesting their meager crops of soy beans and millet in the fall.

Nyu San was less fortunate than his neighbors. Both his parents had died when he was just past boyhood, and he was left to fend for himself. His house, a mud-walled cottage under a thatched roof, stood alone near the edge of a deep fishing pond. Badly in need of repairs, the roof leaked when it rained, the window paper was torn, and the sagging door frame was splin-

---

*An establishment used by government officials for offficial business, and often as a residence.

tered. Behind the house a rickety shed served as a catch-all for tools, fishing nets, and a clutter of rarely used objects. Here, too, Nyu San prepared bean curd to sell in the market place in Dingsyan.

Each morning he rose before dawn, shouldered his carrying pole and walked for one hour until he reached the city. By late afternoon he returned home and started to make ready the next day's batch of curds. After his evening meal, tired and weary, he crawled on top of his *kang** and fell asleep. Thus Nyu San scratched out a living in an endless round of monotonous drudgery. Often he despaired and cursed his fate. By the time he turned twenty-one, he had lost all hope that his lot would improve.

"How can I find a bride?" he grieved. "What woman would be willing to share my broken-down house and the pittance that I earn?"

Unlike the immortals who are given the power to see into the future, Nyu San could not tell beforehand what a strange twist his life would take one early spring day. He had returned from Dingsyan dispirited for he had been unable to sell all of his bean curd. Instead of taking up his usual chores he sat down to rest on a flat rock next to his house. The sun was slowly sinking in the western sky but its lingering rays were warm and comforting, and they made Nyu San drowsy. Before long he nodded off.

Startled out of his nap by the sound of footsteps, he looked up to see a stranger standing at his side.

"Would a tired traveler be able to obtain a bowl of tea?" the man asked politely. "I shall be happy to pay for the refreshment." The offer of payment aroused Nyu San's interest. Fully alert now, he rose and bowed.

"I will not turn away a man in need of so small a favor," he replied.

Seated at Nyu San's table, the stranger sipped the hot tea, smacking his lips after each swallow. He made no effort at con-

---

*A brick platform built across one side of a room, warmed by a fire beneath, and used for sleeping.

versation. Nyu San observed him closely, yet discreetly, not wishing to offend his guest. His robe was of the finest cloth, his hat well made and of a good fit. Envy clutched at Nyu San's heart. A peasant's jacket and trousers made of cheap coarse fabric were the only clothes he had ever owned.

"Are you bound for Dingsyan?" Nyu San asked trying to draw the stranger out.

"Yes, I am a traveling merchant."

"Have you come a long distance?"

"Indeed, yes. I reside in the city of Hangchow."

"Then you must be away from home for long periods of time," Nyu San remarked.

"That is so."

The stranger's reticence was irksome.

"What sort of business do you transact?" Nyu San persisted.

"I deal in silks." The stranger was a little more forthcoming. "I carry my samples with me." He pointed to the pack he had placed on the floor near his chair. "I take orders to be made up for delivery later."

"Surely you grow very tired walking all day with a pack upon your back," offered Nyu San.

"Quite right." With this abrupt reply, the stranger rose.

"Thank you for your hospitality," he said. From a deep pocket in his gown he withdrew a purse, took out a coin and offered it to Nyu San. It did not escape Nyu San's notice that the man's money bag bulged with silver pieces. Envy turned to resentment. But Nyu San's face did not disclose his bitterness. In reply to the stranger's offer of a coin, he bowed low.

"No, no," he protested, "I cannot accept payment for a bowl of tea. It is I who am indebted to you for accepting my modest offering." The stranger stooped to pick up his pack but Nyu San was intent on detaining him.

"If you will not think me too bold, Sir, I would like to suggest that you spend the night under my roof. It is already growing dark. A man of your station, traveling alone, could be waylaid by thieves. Tomorrow morning, after a good night's sleep, you can take up your journey without any thought of danger."

The merchant hesitated. He had often heard stories about bandits who prowled the roads at night looking for likely victims. Besides, he was quite taken in by his host's kindness. "A poor but honest peasant," he thought, "willing to share what little he has."

"Very well," he agreed. "I shall be happy to accept your gracious offer."

Nyu San prepared a simple evening meal of noodles and boiled cabbage. The stranger ate heartily. As soon as he had emptied his bowl he put down his chopsticks, expressed his thanks again, and declared that he would like to retire early since he wished to arrive in Dingsyan the next day well before noon.

"You will be quite comfortable on the *kang*," Nyu San assured him. "I, too, must rise before the first cock crow but I cannot retire just now for there are a few chores to which I must attend." He bade the stranger good night and stepped out of the house.

The air had a sharp bite to it. A few stars twinkled among the scudding clouds. A sliver of moon hung in the sky providing just enough light for Nyu San to walk about without stumbling. Never, in all his days, had he felt so miserable.

"Life is unbearably cruel," Nyu San lamented. "I have slaved for so many years and have nothing. This fellow's hands are soft and white. He has probably never done a day's hard labor, yet he lives like a prince." Nyu San cursed his destiny and railed against heaven itself for permitting such an injustice. His anger mounted to an irrepressible fury. He made a fateful decision.

When he thought that enough time had elapsed for the stranger to have fallen asleep, Nyu San slipped back into the house. He stood just inside the door listening to the merchant's rhythmic breathing. Nyu San reached for an old worn work jacket that hung on a nearby peg. On cat's feet he crept toward the sleeping figure curled up on the *kang*. Suddenly the stranger rolled over on his back. Nyu San stiffened. The stranger slumbered on, snoring loudly. His heart racing wildly, his mouth dry as desert sand, Nyu San tiptoed closer until he stood over the man's head. Lunging forward, he clamped the quilted jacket over the stranger's face and held it down tightly, pressing as hard as he was able. For a few agonizing minutes the victim struggled. It seemed an eternity before his body went limp and his breathing ceased.

Nyu San backed away slowly. He was trembling. A wave of remorse swept over him.

"I have killed a man," he whispered hoarsely.

Paralyzed with fear, his mind did not yet contemplate what would happen if he were found out. For a long time he did not stir. Slowly, the enormity of the peril that awaited him became clear. He had to get rid of the body!

In a frenzy he ran to the shed behind his house. Near the back wall he could make out a pair of old worn-down millstones that had long been out of use. He picked up the smaller top stone, carried it out of the shed and lifted it onto a flat barrow. Then he dashed back into the house. Never expecting the body to be so unwieldy, he struggled to drag it outside. With a grunt he heaved it over the millstone. The head lolled to one side and the hands hung down limply.

Nyu San rummaged around in an old reed basket. From amidst the jumble, he pulled out a short length of sturdy rope. "It will have to do," he decided.

He tied the stranger's feet together with one end. The other end he threaded through the hole in the center of the millstone, securing it with several tight knots. Unmindful of the heavy load, he pulled the barrow toward a section of the fishing pond where the ground fell away sharply. Here he knew the water to be deepest. Turning the barrow full around he edged it toward the bank. A wave of nausea swept over him. With a grunt he upended the barrow. The weighted body slid off and sank to the muddy bottom making hardly a splash. Nyu San prayed the pond would keep his secret forever.

Not wishing to arouse the curiosity of his neighbors, Nyu San used his ill-begotten wealth prudently. Enriched with the stranger's silver, he gradually began to make bigger purchases of soy beans and double his output of bean curd. No longer did he have to walk to the market place in Dingsyan. Instead, he hitched his newly acquired donkey to a two-wheeled cart to make his daily rounds. Little by little he set about repairing his cottage and adding to its simple furnishings.

The following year he married a girl from a nearby village. Lingling's parents were pleased with the wedding gifts their son-in-law presented to them. They considered him a man of means who would be able to take care of their daughter, and they were not disappointed. In time, Nyu San added another room to his house in anticipation that his family would grow. How delighted he was when Lingling gave birth to a son! The happy father dreamed of a day when little Ahu would be able to work at his side, and took comfort knowing that when he and Lingling grew old, there would be someone to care for them.

Though good fortune dulls the memory of past troubles, Nyu San could never entirely banish from his thoughts the stranger who, by some trick of fate, had entered his life. Nor could he, after that fateful night, walk near the pond without feeling his heart begin to pound and his chest constrict with pain. But with each passing day the memory grew dimmer and dimmer.

Twenty years of peace and contentment followed one upon the other until Nyu San became aware of encroaching age. His hair was peppered with gray, his gait slower, and less steady. He preferred to putter about and take a nap in the afternoon leaving Ahu to attend to the job of preparing and selling the bean curd.

It was at this time that the young Lord Bau was appointed judge for Dingsyan city. He came to his new position determined to carry out his duties faithfully and to serve the Emperor as a trusted officer. A man of high ideals, he pledged to himself that he would treat rich and poor alike, honestly and fairly. During the early weeks in his new post he acquainted himself with his administrative duties and arranged comfortable quarters for his two aides, Wang Chau and Ma Han.

On the first inspection tour of his prefecture, Lord Bau arrived at Nyu San's village. Judging by the shabby appearance of the houses, he understood that those who lived there were not prosperous. But all seemed orderly and tranquil as he strolled through the winding streets accompanied by his aides. At the eastern end of the village, a dirt path veered off the main road to circle around a pond. The three men had continued along the path only a short distance when they stopped to watch a group of five young boys engaged in a game of water tag. Splashing about good-naturedly they dove beneath the surface, came up for air, shook their heads to shed a shower of drops, before disappearing from sight again. The noisy play ended abruptly when one of the boys rose out of the water holding a skull in one hand. His companions followed him to the shore where they gathered around, staring with awe at the bone white object with its empty eye sockets and yellowed teeth. They were soon joined by Lord Bau and his aides.

"Where did you find that?" asked Lord Bau of the boy who had made the discovery.

"My hand brushed against something hard when I dove down. I was curious and reached for it."

"Some poor soul must have drowned long ago," thought Lord Bau. Silently, he began to mull over how it could have happened. An accident? Perhaps. Suicide? Foul play?

"Since you are such an excellent swimmer," remarked Lord Bau, addressing the young diver, "would you be willing to look for some other hard objects in the area where you found the skull? I shall be glad to pay for any you can retrieve."

"We are good swimmers, too," chimed in his friends eager to share the benefits of Lord Bau's offer.

Lord Bau smiled. "Agreed. Anyone who brings up a hard object will be rewarded."

Laughing and shouting the boys plunged into the water. As Lord Bau suspected, the skull had not lain in its watery grave unaccompanied. Before long the boys recovered several bleached bones. To everyone's surprise, the last boy to come ashore brought up a flat rounded stone with a hole in the center. "See what I have found," he called out, holding the encrusted find aloft with both hands.

The boys were sent away happily, each fingering a coin. Lord Bau instructed his aides to carry the skeletal remains and the small round stone back to the *yamen* for closer inspection.

An astute observer, Lord Bau studied the strange articles for several days. From the size of the skull and the bones, he was reasonably certain that they were those of a grown male. Their condition indicated that they had been submerged for a very long time. As for the stone, it was without doubt, a millstone such as is commonly found in most homes, one used to grind small amounts of grain for daily use. The proximity of the skeleton and the millstone at the bottom of the pond suggested foul play. The killer had weighted his victim's body with the millstone before disposing of it in the water. To prove his theory might be difficult if not impossible, but Lord Bau felt duty-bound to unravel the mystery.

"Before I begin my investigation," Lord Bau told his aides, "the poor fellow deserves a proper burial no matter how he may have departed the earth." Ma Han and Wang Chau arranged for the skeletal remains to be laid to rest according to ritual, and for the erection of a memorial tablet, bearing the simple inscription, THE TOMB OF AN UNKNOWN SOUL.

All through the following week, Lord Bau spent many hours poring over old records. Not a single report of a missing person could he find. The dead man, he reasoned, had not been a resident of his prefecture. More likely, he was a stranger passing through who had met with some extraordinary accident. The identity of his killer might never be established. After much pondering, Lord Bau decided to gamble on one clue, the top half of the small reddish millstone.

Ma Han and Wang Chau were summoned to his office and handed packets of notices with instructions to display them throughout Dingsyan and all the neighboring villages. "Secure them to the trees along the roads, post them on building walls, attach them to gateposts," they were told. The posters bore the following message:

> All millstones brought to the *yamen* gate
> Will be paid for according to weight.

Old ones, small ones will be accepted,
New ones, large ones will be rejected.
Bring top stones, bottom stones or a pair,
No matter the condition of wear.

"But Master," protested Ma Han, "why do you wish to collect millstones? Surely, you are not thinking of grinding and selling grain."

"Are you about to open a shop to repair old millstones?" added Wang Chau.

"Your questions are tiresome," replied Lord Bau. "All I ask for is your cooperation. The reason for my instructions will become evident later on. When people bring their millstones, be sure to keep a record of the name and address of each donor. Weigh every stone carefully and pay strictly according to weight."

In the courtyard of the *yamen*, Ma Han and Wang Chau suspended a large steelyard from a protruding roof beam. It was not long before people streamed in from all parts of the prefecture. They lugged millstones in baskets hung from the ends of poles, they pulled them in hand-drawn carts, they tied them to the backs of donkeys. To each stone Ma Han and Wang Chau affixed a piece of cotton paper bearing the name of its owner and his place of residence. Just before sunset every day, Lord Bau inspected the latest arrivals.

By the end of two weeks, hundreds of stones had been stacked in neat piles. Some were worn thin by years of use, others broken in half. A few were covered with mold from being left on the damp ground for years. But all were of the same dull gray shade. Lord Bau was beginning to feel disheartened. The specific stone that he hoped would turn up was not there.

On the second day of the third week, something caught Lord Bau's eye. Were he not so alert, he could easily have missed the small red millstone tucked between two larger ones. At once he had it carried back to his office. When it proved to be a perfect match to the one that had been taken from the pond, he beamed

From all parts of the prefecture, people arrived
bearing millstones.

with satisfaction. The owner, as recorded on the list prepared by his aides, was one Nyu Ahu.

Within the hour, Lord Bau's aides were dispatched to Nyu Ahu's cottage.

"Is this the home of Nyu Ahu?" inquired Ma Han when the door was opened by an elderly man.

"He is my son," replied Nyu San gesturing toward the young man seated at the kitchen table.

"We place him under arrest on orders of Lord Bau."

"There must be some mistake," Nyu San protested strongly. "My son has done nothing wrong."

"That is not for you to say. If he were innocent of wrongdoing, Lord Bau would not have sent for him."

Without further explanation, Ma Han and Wang Chau pushed Nyu San aside and made straight for the bewildered Ahu. They tied his hands behind his back and marched him away.

Nyu San staggered back to his seat, his legs almost giving way beneath him.

In the presence of Lord Bau, Ahu, utterly perplexed by the turn of events, knew not what to expect. Lord Bau's questions were clipped and direct.

"State your full name."

"Nyu Ahu, Your Honor."

"Name the members of your family."

"My father is Nyu San, my mother is Lingling."

"What is your age?"

"In the coming year of the rat I shall attain my twentieth birthday."

Lord Bau rose from his chair. Slowly he walked back and forth behind his desk.

"Where did you find the millstone you brought to the *yamen* in exchange for money?" he asked.

Still confused but a little more at ease, Ahu explained. "It has been in our shed for as long as I can remember. Since my family had no use for it, I did not think anyone would object to my exchanging it for a few pieces of cash."

"Did you ask your father's permission to remove the millstone?"

"No, Honorable Sir. As I have already explained, I did not think he would object. Besides, the top half was missing. The bottom half was useless without it."

"I see," said Lord Bau. He stopped his pacing and faced Ahu. "We have evidence to suggest that a murder was committed and that your stone may have played a part in the crime."

"Sir, I humbly beg your pardon, but if you think that I or anyone else in my family could be guilty of such a dreadful deed, you are mistaken. We are honest and law abiding people, known throughout our village to be hard working and respectable."

"The evidence weighs heavily against you," Lord Bau replied. He watched Ahu's face for any reaction to his words. Ahu, eyebrows furrowed, mouth agape, regarded his accuser with disbelief.

"Until the case can be resolved," Lord Bau continued, "I must detain you."

That night, sleep would not come to Ahu's father. Nyu San tossed miserably until the first light of dawn. He dressed quickly and left his house, walking swiftly in the direction of Dingsyan. Determined to discover the reason for his son's arrest, he would seek an audience with Lord Bau.

"I have been expecting you," said Lord Bau after Nyu San was ushered into his study. "You see," he added without wasting words, "the skeleton of a murdered man and the top half of a millstone were recently recovered from the pond in your village. I have been anxious to locate the matching bottom half of that stone in the hope that it may lead me to the killer. Yesterday it was turned in by your son who is now being held on suspicion of murder. If found guilty, he will be put to death."

Nyu San felt the room and everything in it begin to spin around his head.

"In a moment," he thought, "I shall lose consciousness and disgrace myself."

"Can you offer some explanation to prove your son's innocence?" asked Lord Bau. Nyu San merely shook his head.

"Then you are excused," Lord Bau said. "You may leave."

"I b-b-beg Your Honor, have mercy," Nyu San stammered before being led out of the room.

Lord Bau was usually more thorough in his interrogations. His aides Ma Han and Wang Chau were quite taken aback when, upon Nyu San's departure, Lord Bau ordered them to post notices of a public execution to take place on the first day of the new month.

"But Master, are you convinced that the young man we arrested is guilty?" asked Ma Han.

"He is not guilty!" came the startling reply.

"Then surely, you are not going to take the life of an innocent person?" said Wang Chau.

"To catch a big fish, one must use the proper bait." Lord Bau had the annoying habit of offering a proverb in place of a direct answer.

On the first day of the new month, an hour before noon, throngs of people had already filled the street in front of the *yamen*. Still more kept coming, pushing and jostling for a good position. The block on which the condemned prisoner would place his head had been set in place and the area around it cordoned off. The long curved knife, hinged to one side of the block was in an upright position and its polished surface shone with an eerie brilliance. Yet to make his appearance was the executioner.

Just before noon, a gong was struck—three loud hammer blows. The chilling sound reverberated, hung in the air for a moment, then gradually faded away. The *yamen* gates opened and the executioner stepped forth wearing a black-belted tunic. At his side walked a drummer beating a slow steady rhythm. In measured steps the executioner solemnly approached the block. Again, the gong struck, sending out a wave of nerve-shattering sound, and once more the *yamen* gate opened. Lord Bau emerged, dressed in his silk brocade ceremonial gown. Walking with dignity in time to the drum beat, he took his position behind the executioner. At a sign, the drum was stilled.

"Bring out the prisoner," thundered Lord Bau. A hush deeper than the silence of the grave descended over the throng. The drum resumed its melancholy beat. For the third time the *yamen* gate opened. Flanked by Ma Han and Wang Chau, Ahu was brought forward in a slotted prisoner's wagon. Suddenly, a pitiable wail arose from the midst of the assembled multitude.

"Ay, ay, he is innocent, he is innocent, do not kill him, he is innocent!" Pushing his way through the onlookers was a disheveled man intoning the same dolorous phrase over and over. A crazed Nyu San threw himself at Lord Bau's feet. He *kowtowed**, beating his head repeatedly against the ground until blood ran freely down his cheeks.

"Your Honor," he sobbed, "I am the guilty one. I am the murderer!"

"We have our big fish," Lord Bau whispered aside to his aides. "Set the boy free."

Nyu San was placed in a cell to await sentencing. Grim thoughts crowded into his head. What he feared most was not dying, for he expected to be punished in accordance with the principle that he who take another's life, pays with his own. Rather, he worried that Ahu, as the son of a murderer, would forever after be tainted. What a dreadful legacy to leave his only child!

From the long strip of woven cloth wound twice around his waist to hold up his trousers, Nyu San fashioned a noose. The next morning he was found hanging from a rafter.

Later Lord Bau's curious aides posed some questions.

"Why were you so certain," asked Ma Han, "that the son, Ahu, was blameless?"

"If your eyes were sharper and your brain keener," Lord Bau told him, "you would have been able to figure it out yourself." Patiently, he explained. "From the condition of the skeleton and the millstone taken from the pond it was obvious that they had

---

*To kneel and touch forehead to the ground in a token of homage or deep respect.

"Ay, ay, do not kill him, he is innocent."

been under water for many years. Our young prisoner was not even born when the murder was committed.

Wang Chau wondered aloud, "What are we going to do with all those millstones you collected?"

Lord Bau's eyes twinkled, and he had a ready answer. "The millstones will make excellent paving material for the street in front of the *yamen*. Do you not agree it will be an improvement over the dusty, pockmarked roadway that so many people must pass over?" His aides nodded in agreement. "Good, then conscript enough men to do the job under your supervision."

Ma Han and Wang Chau had not bargained for such an assignment, but they dared not refuse Lord Bau's bidding. The work proceeded without delay. There were enough gray millstones to pave the short street from one end to the other. The small red millstone, the clue that helped to solve the mystery of the submerged skeleton, was given the place of honor in the center of the street.

The True Mother

Hai-tang was fourteen when her father, with no outward sign of illness, suddenly died. The scholarly Jang Yu had paid little attention to matters of money, preferring to spend his time immersed in the books of the great sages. Having failed to lay aside even the smallest sum against adversity, his family was left in dire straits.

To his sixteen-year-old son, Jang Lin, fell the responsibility of providing for his mother and sister, but the boy was ill-prepared to take his place as head of the household. From early childhood he had shown no inclination for learning. Even more disappointing to his parents, Jang Lin was possessed of a selfish, disagreeable nature. Without special skills he was not suited for any occupation other than menial jobs, but he refused any offers that entailed much hard labor for very little pay. Finally he became discouraged and refused to look for work any longer. His widowed mother was beside herself with worry. She and her children faced the prospect of starvation.

With her family's survival threatened, Madam Jang reluctantly, and with a heavy heart, considered a way out of their troubles, a remedy that would have been unthinkable in other circumstances.

"Hai-tang is young and pretty," she reflected. "Men will pay well for her company. The money she can bring home will tide us over until better times." The agonizing decision was made. At a still tender age, Hai-tang became a prostitute, the mainstay of her family.

Jang Lin enjoyed the full rice bowl that his sister's earnings provided. Yet he showed not the least appreciation. Full of resentment, he berated her at every opportunity.

"You are nothing but cheap trash. You have humiliated me before my friends and disgraced our good name," he would often rail. "Better that you had died in place of our father. Now we are stained with your shame because you sell your body for a few filthy coins."

"The fault is not mine, elder brother," Hai-tang tried to appease him. "We have suffered through hard times since father departed this life. Were it not for the money I earn, and it is little enough, we would all go hungry." Rarely did Hai-tang raise her voice against Jang Lin's painful accusations. Her brother was quick-tempered, prone to use his fists when crossed. At times even a mild response would touch off an unbridled explosion of temper. More than once Jang Lin had delivered a slap to Hai-tang's cheek that sent her reeling. Though she burned with indignation she had learned to hold her tongue.

"How dare he reproach me when it is I who am making all the sacrifices," she thought. "He fritters away the days in idleness and has failed in his filial duty to look after our mother."

Nor did Madam Jang come to her daughter's defense during these stormy exchanges. Afraid to antagonize her son further, she cowered in a corner waiting for his outbursts to subside.

Jang Lin's fits of rage had been happening with increasing frequency. Like a volcano, his anger smoldered until it erupted without control.

One day, after a bitter argument with Hai-tang, he shouted angrily, "I'm leaving, I'm leaving for the city this very moment. There's work to be found there, decent work, not the dirty labor that reduces a man to a slaving drudge. Away from this place I shall be free of the taint of our cursed family."

Without a word of farewell, Jang Lin stormed out of the house, but not before he had turned on Hai-tang once more.

"You are to take care of our mother," he warned, "or you will have to answer to me. If you fail to provide for her, I shall see to it that you never again enjoy a peaceful day." Mother and daughter sought to comfort each other in a tearful embrace.

Misfortune's bitter fruit may sometimes unexpectedly turn sweet. Hai-tang had been compelled to become a prostitute when her father died. Yet, had she not been forced to degrade herself, she would never have met Officer Ma.

He had come to the brothel one evening seeking more pleasant companionship than he could expect from his sullen wife. As soon as Hai-tang was presented to him, he sensed that she was quite extraordinary. Her refined speech and girlish shyness appealed to him. After that, he came often to be entertained, spending the night in her company. So enamored of her did Ma become, he offered to take Hai-tang as his second wife. She, in turn, was thrilled with the prospect of release from her shameful way of life.

"Your kindness, Sir, makes me happier than you can imagine. I have no father," she told him, "so you must seek the permission of my mother. She depends upon me for her support and I shall not be able to abandon her."

Ma assured Hai-tang he could overcome any objections her mother might pose.

"Just arrange a suitable time for me to pay her a visit. I shall quiet any doubts she may have."

Madam Jang greeted Officer Ma with formal politeness when he came to call on her. She observed that he was considerably older than Hai-tang though still attractive. Tall and straight, with regular features and thick black hair, his appearance belied his age. Yet she still harbored some reservations. Her daughter would be a concubine, subject to the whims of Ma's first wife. And if Hai-tang were to leave home, Madam Jang would be left alone without any means of income.

Ma anticipated Madam Jang's hesitation. She seemed embarrassed. She did not wish to offend.

"Who will look after me when Hai-tang is gone?" she asked

timidly. "And your first wife, how can I be certain she will not mistreat my daughter?"

Officer Ma waved her objections aside. "I will send you money enough for your needs. You shall want for nothing. As for my first wife, I will see to it that she treats Hai-tang like a sister."

Hai-tang, who had discreetly kept her silence during the conversation between Madam Jang and Officer Ma, smiled with delight when her mother gave her consent. To become the wife of this good man, to be respected and loved, what more could a girl in her circumstances ask for?

When her husband informed her he was taking a concubine, Precious Pearl was not upset. Her status as first wife remained secure. Rather than consider Hai-tang a threat, she secretly welcomed the new arrangement. Precious Pearl had a lover by the name of Jao, a minor official in the government of nearby Jeng City. It would be to her advantage to have her husband distracted by his young concubine, leaving her free to arrange clandestine meetings with Jao.

Within the year, Hai-tang gave birth to a male child. Ma showered her with gifts, so happy was he to have a son. Precious Pearl masked her feelings of jealousy. For the next four years, pretending to be on the best of terms with Hai-tang, both women raised little Ping together.

The tragic events that followed may have been averted if Jao had not tired of sharing Precious Pearl with Officer Ma. A time came when he reminded her that they were both growing older and they should wait no longer.

"Let us flee," he urged. "I can find work in another city. Why should we be kept apart, always having to put up a false front and hiding our true feelings?"

Precious Pearl was wary of taking so bold a step. Jao's earnings would probably be insufficient to permit her the very comfortable life she enjoyed. She did not wish to make a foolish blunder by acting in haste. At the same time, she realized she would not be able to put Jao off forever. She begged him to wait just a little longer.

"Do not despair, there may be another way out of our predicament."

For the moment, she was able to placate him. When next Precious Pearl stole away to meet Jao she gave him some money with instructions to buy a vial of strong poison at the apothecary shop. Jao was alarmed, but Precious Pearl made light of his protests.

"Trust me, all will be well," she promised. "Before many moons have waxed and waned we shall be together forever." Obedient to her wishes, Jao purchased the vial of poison and gave it to her.

Scheming all the while to get rid of Ma, Precious Pearl bided her time. She would wait for the right opportunity to present itself. It came on the day Ping turned five.

Precious Pearl and Ma left with the child at mid-morning to burn incense at the temple in honor of his birthday. Hai-tang remained at home to prepare a special feast of which they would all partake that evening.

Hai-tang put on her prettiest dress and anxiously awaited her family's return. The table had been laid with the finest wine cups. Near each cup Hai-tang had placed a set of ivory chopsticks. She was admiring the lovely arrangements when a servant announced the arrival of an unexpected caller. Hai-tang wondered who the stranger could be. He was dressed in tattered garments, and except that he held himself proudly, she might have mistaken him for a beggar. Not until he spoke her name did she recognize her own brother, Jang Lin.

"What brings you to my door after so long an absence?" she asked in astonishment. Plainly embarrassed, Jang Lin squirmed and hesitated before answering.

"I am reduced to desperate circumstances, else I would not be here to intrude on your happy life. When I left home for the capital, I had hoped to find lodgings with our uncle. Unhappily, upon arrival at his house I learned that he was no longer alive. For many years I struggled, earning barely enough to get by. Then I took ill and could not continue to work. There was nowhere for me to turn but home. To my sorrow, I found that our dear mother had died in my absence and that you had married the wealthy Officer Ma. I throw myself at your mercy. Please, dear sister, do not turn me away."

Jang Lin seemed so dejected, Hai-tang felt a momentary twinge of pity. But it was only a fleeting tug at her heart. Painful remembrances came flooding back. She could not help throwing up to him his past abuse.

"You ran off to the city without regard for our mother, and now you dare to appear uninvited to plead for help!"

"I ask for very little, only enough to buy a new gown," Jang Lin said meekly. "I am on my way to Kaifeng. There, if I am dressed properly and make a good appearance, I will surely be able to find a suitable position. Though I am not a scholar, I can read and write and know how to use an abacus. Someone will find my services valuable and hire me."

"I own nothing in this house. I have nothing to give." Hai-tang hoped her curt reply would be understood as a dismissal, that Jang Lin would take it with the finality that she intended.

Jang Lin persisted.

"I did not expect such cruelty from my own sister. If you are not willing to help me, I shall wait until Officer Ma returns home. He has the reputation of being a charitable man."

"Do as you please!" Hai-tang left the room, slamming the door behind her.

Jang Lin did not have long to wait. But it was not Officer Ma who entered the guest hall. It was a woman leading a small tired boy by the hand.

Startled by the presence of someone she had never laid eyes on before, Precious Pearl cried out in alarm. "Who are you and what are you doing here?"

"I mean no harm." Jang Lin bowed deeply. "I am the elder brother of Hai-tang. I have come to call on my sister."

"Then why is she not with you? And why," she added, "do you appear clad in rags?" Precious Pearl regarded him with disgust.

"I ask your forgiveness, Madam. I have not been well for many months, unable to work, and my money has run out. Now that I have recovered, it is my intention to journey to the capital to seek employment. As you can see, it would not do to appear before a prospective employer improperly attired. I have come to ask my sister for a small loan, only enough to buy some suitable clothing. Alas, she has hardened her heart and refused me. I have no alternative but to humble myself by appealing to the generosity of Officer Ma."

Precious Pearl was quick to see that the quarrel between brother and sister could be used to her own advantage.

She sent the child away in the care of a maid. Then she turned her attention to Jang Lin.

"Why did she refuse you? Her own brother!"

"She said that she owned nothing, and, therefore, had nothing to give."

"What nonsense!" snapped Precious Pearl. "Wait here. I may be able to persuade her to change her mind."

Precious Pearl found Hai-tang resting in her room.

"Dear sister," she said most tenderly, "I have just met your brother. He has laid bare his heart to me. Do you not think it cruel to deny him a few pieces of cash when he asks for so little? I have never known you to be so unfeeling."

"My brother does not merit any kindness from me," Hai-tang answered coldly.

"But your brother is part of our family. You would not turn away a stranger. How is it that you show no mercy for a blood relative?"

Precious Pearl's words shamed Hai-tang.

"But I have no money to give him," she protested.

"You can offer him something that can be exchanged for money. Why not give him your lovely dress? It will bring a goodly sum."

Hai-tang considered the suggestion.

"I would gladly part with my dress, but when the master returns and notices that I am not wearing it, he will question me. I am afraid he will be very cross when he thinks I have chosen to wear my ordinary clothes for our son's birthday celebration."

"You need not worry about that. I shall speak up for you," Precious Pearl promised.

Trustingly, Hai-tang removed her silk dress. She folded it with care and handed it to Precious Pearl. Along with it, as an extra gesture of good will, she added a silver necklace.

"Do not trouble yourself further," Precious Pearl told her. "I shall see that your brother receives your generous offering and send him on his way."

It was quite another picture that Precious Pearl painted for Jang Lin. "Your sister is ill-natured and selfish," she lied. "I could not convince her to part with any of her belongings. Her stubbornness is beyond my understanding. To deny a small charity to a kinsman in need is against my nature. Please accept my dress," she said, pretending earnestness and affection while pressing Hai-tang's package into his hands. "It is similar to Hai-tang's and just as valuable. My wish is that you have good luck and happier days."

The smirk of satisfaction had not yet left Precious Pearl's face when Officer Ma returned home.

"You must be very tired," Precious Pearl said. "I did not expect you to remain so long at the temple."

Pleased with his wife's unusually warm greeting, Ma told her he had noticed some slight damage to the temple wall and had taken it upon himself to repair the fallen stones.

Hai-tang overheard the voices and knew her husband was back. She came to welcome him, carrying a bowl of hot soup.

"Master, I have prepared your favorite dish." She placed the steaming soup before Ma, who had taken his seat at the table. "I trust you will like it," she added cheerfully, hoping that he would not notice the old dress she was wearing. Just as Ma reached to pick up the bowl, Precious Pearl snatched it away and brought it to her lips. She took one sip and turned up her nose.

"This will never do," she declared. "The soup is tasteless, it lacks salt. I'll fix it just the way you like it." She strode out of the room so quickly neither Hai-tang nor Ma could protest.

Precious Pearl returned and set the bowl of soup before her husband. "You will like it better now," she said, urging him to drink. But Officer Ma paid no attention to the soup. His eyes were fixed on Hai-tang. "Why are you not wearing your beautiful new dress? Is not our son's fifth birthday cause for celebration?"

"Forgive me, Master. Our son's birthday is always a joyful day, but I can explain." Hai-tang felt the blood rush to her face. "Today, my brother came to visit me unexpectedly and asked for . . . "

"It was not her brother," broke in Precious Pearl. "Hai-tang has no brother, only a lover," she sneered. "She gave him her clothes to sell in the marketplace because they are planning to run away together."

Officer Ma's mouth fell open. "Hai-tang, does Precious Pearl speak the truth?" he demanded, eyes wide with astonishment.

"No, no, Master. It is not so. I have no lover. Please believe me. The visitor was my own brother. He came to beg me for help." Hai-tang glared at Precious Pearl. "Sister, what has happened between us? Why are you making up these falsehoods?"

"What can one expect from a former prostitute but a pack of lies?" Precious Pearl looked past Hai-tang and addressed Officer Ma. "Master, it is not the first time your second wife has had a lover. There have been many others before this one. I have seen her sneak them into the house whenever you are away."

Officer Ma flew into a rage. He grabbed Hai-tang by the shoulders and shook her without mercy. Savagely, he threw her to the floor. He sank into his chair and buried his face in his arms.

"Do taste the soup while it is still hot," Precious Pearl urged again. "It will restore your strength and calm your nerves." The saccharine words dripped from her lips.

Officer Ma, still confused and distraught, drank deeply. Precious Pearl observed him anxiously while the insidious poison coursed through his veins. Officer Ma's face turned purple, the bowl slid from his hands, crashing to the floor. His eyes rolled back into his head. His limp body slid off the chair. Crumpled

The bowl slide from his hands, crashing to the floor.
His eyes rolled back into his head.

and lifeless, he lay on the floor.

Hai-tang kneeled at his side. Cradling Ma's head in her arms, she rocked back and forth wailing, "Master, why have you left us? How can we live without you? Who will be a father to our son?"

Precious Pearl pulled Hai-tang away from Ma's body. "Murderess!" she shrieked. "Why do you shed false tears? It is you who killed him. You must have poisoned the soup!"

Hai-tang rose to her feet. Her eyes were red-rimmed, her face ashen. For the first time she dared to confront Precious Pearl. She chose every word deliberately. "You tasted the soup I prepared and suffered no harm. Your treachery becomes clear to me now. On the pretext that the soup lacked salt, you took the bowl into the kitchen. But you did not add salt. You added poison instead. You, and you alone, killed Ma."

"No one will ever be able to prove that," shot back Precious Pearl. "If you accuse me, it will be the word of a concubine against the word of a first wife. You are nothing but a lowborn whore whose vile reputation follows you wherever you go. How will you ever be able to convince anyone that you are innocent? Besides," Precious Pearl threatened, "I will bear witness against you and never rest until you are punished. But first I must arrange for my husband's funeral."

Both Precious Pearl and Hai-tang, clad in white mourning garments, wept at Officer Ma's grave. Out of respect for the dead, they did not quarrel on the day of the funeral or during the seven weeks of mourning. But the peace between them could not last. Hai-tang was so wounded by Precious Pearl's falseness she decided to have nothing more to do with her. The hurt was particularly deep since she had once considered Precious Pearl as a sister. She knew that she could not remain in the same house with this crafty schemer who had become her mortal enemy.

Hai-tang informed Precious Pearl of her decision to leave with her son. She would take only their personal possessions. She asked for nothing else nor expected any favors.

Precious Pearl's reply was as a knife thrust into Hai-tang's chest.

"You may go, but you must leave the boy with me. Do you

think that I am fool enough to let Ma's sole heir slip from my grasp? He and all of his father's wealth will be mine."

Hai-tang regarded Precious Pearl with loathing.

"Never, never will I give up my son. Never will I leave him with one as evil as you."

"You really have no choice," sneered Precious Pearl with cold, deliberate malice. "We can settle the matter in either of two ways, privately between the two of us, or publicly in court before a judge. If you agree to leave without the boy, I shall promise never to speak to anyone of how you killed Ma. If you choose to settle the matter publicly, I shall bring charges against you. Not only will I accuse you of murder but also of trying to steal my son."

Aghast at Precious Pearl's cunning, Hai-tang realized that a trap had been laid for her. If it were only her life that was being threatened, she would not have resisted Precious Pearl's will. But her son's future was at stake. She vowed to fight back.

"Your dastardly scheme will not succeed. Where my son is concerned I shall have the upper hand." Hai-tang became bolder.

"All the neighbors know that you are barren. The midwife who was present at my delivery will tell which one of us is the true mother."

Precious Pearl laughed aloud. "You are a greater fool than I thought you were. It will take only the smell of money to bribe the whole lot. At the sight of a few pieces of silver their tongues will twist according to my instructions. They will swear that I gave birth to the boy."

"I will take my chances in court before I surrender my child."

Hai-tang held firm. Nor did she budge when Precious Pearl attempted to intimidate her.

"I can hear your screams as they beat a confession out of you. You will gladly admit that you murdered Officer Ma when you can no longer bear the pain. After you are sentenced to death, your son will be left an orphan in my care. What will you have gained? Nothing!"

"I'll not confess to something I did not do," Hai-tang said simply.

Hai-tang's defiance infuriated Precious Pearl. Now she determined to accuse Hai-tang of murder before the local authorities. She turned all her efforts to concocting an airtight scenario, schooling the witnesses to lie when questioned, and rehearsing how to play the role of the aggrieved widow. When asked to testify she would remind the officers of Hai-tang's sordid past. Hai-tang stood little chance of receiving an impartial hearing, for one of the local officers who would sit in judgment was none other than Precious Pearl's lover, Jao. Having supplied the poison that was slipped into Officer Ma's soup, Jao would take particular care not to implicate himself. Precious Pearl felt secure that Jao would play his part cautiously.

From the outset, Hai-tang's declaration of innocence was completely ignored. Jao questioned the witnesses. Neighbor after neighbor and the midwife swore the child belonged to Precious Pearl. All of Hai-tang's protestations were cut short, and, finally, when she refused to admit her guilt, Jao directed that she be beaten. The lashing was brutal.

"Confess, confess," Jao demanded in response to Hai-tang's screams of pain. The wretched Hai-tang succumbed to the agonizing torment. All hope lost, she cried out that she had poisoned her husband and plotted to steal Precious Pearl's son.

The local authorities had the power to hear cases but could not mete out sentences. This fell within the duties of the head judge in the county capital.

It was arranged that Hai-tang be escorted to Kaifeng where Lord Bau, the presiding judge, would pass sentence. Jao prepared a complete report of the case. Attached to it was Hai-tang's duly signed confession. Her conviction was assured. Of this Jao felt confident.

On the day Hai-tang was being escorted to Kaifeng, the weather was bitterly cold. A snow squall blew down from the bleak sky, covering the earth with a white blanket. For Hai-tang, weak from the beating she had sustained, each step was agony. She was not alone in her misery. Her escorts, buffeted by the cutting, icy winds, shivered in their quilted cotton clothes. What a welcome pleasure it was when they came upon a wine shop and entered its warm, noisy interior.

The numbness leaving their frozen fingers and toes stung like needle pricks. They had only begun to thaw out when the door blew open and another customer entered. He sat down at a table near theirs and called for a bowl of warm wine. Hai-tang soon noticed that the newcomer was staring at her. After he was served, he continued to gaze at her over the edge of his bowl. Hai-tang averted her eyes, embarrassed by the stranger's interest. Yet, she sensed a vague glimmer of recognition. Something about him was familiar. She dared to peek at him again and found that he was observing her with a quizzical look on his face. Awareness dawned on them both at the same instant. She had not recognized her brother for he wore the gown of a court official, and Jang Lin had not imagined the disheveled, bruised woman to be his lovely sister.

Their first exchange of words was halting. Jang Lin recalled how Hai-tang had rejected his plea for help and did not know whether she still bore a grudge against him. Hai-tang considered her brother's appearance at this, her time of need, no less than a miracle, but she wondered if he would ever forgive her past selfishness. Gradually, they warmed toward one another, exchanging news about what had happened to them since their last unfortunate meeting. For the first time, Jang Lin was made aware of the truth. The clothes and necklace he had received were not Precious Pearl's but those of his sister.

How strange are the turns of fate! Jang Lin also learned that Hai-tang was a prisoner about to appear before Lord Bau for sentencing, while Hai-tang learned that Jang Lin was now employed as a member of Lord Bau's staff.

Jang Lin consoled Hai-tang and held out some hope for her.

"You have been wronged, dear sister. I can understand your suffering, and I will stand by you until you are vindicated. When you are called upon," he instructed, "tell Lord Bau exactly what happened. He never fails to separate truth from falsehood. He will see through Precious Pearl's wily tricks."

In his usual thorough manner, Lord Bau carefully reviewed Precious Pearl's charges against Hai-tang. He concluded that far from being an open and shut case, the testimony presented merited further scrutiny because several points needed clarification. It was not uncommon for an immoral concubine to kill her husband, but why should she want to steal the first wife's child? He also wished to take more time to reexamine the facts relating to the poisoned soup. There was still a motive to be established. And what of the lover? His identity had to be confirmed. He, too, had to be questioned.

Lord Bau chose first to settle the conflict between the two women to determine who was the child's true mother. He summoned an aide to his side and whispered in his ear. The aide left the courtroom, returning a few moments later with a bucket of ground limestone in one hand, a trowel in the other. Methodically he sprinkled the limestone powder on the floor, creating a circle about five feet in diameter. Then he marked the center of the circle clearly.

"Rise," Lord Bau commanded. Precious Pearl and Hai-tang rose to their feet.

"Is the boy in the courtroom?"

"He is, Honorable Lord," they answered in unison.

"Bring him forward and stand him in the center of the circle." Hai-tang and Precious Pearl obeyed.

"Each of you is to grasp the boy by a hand and try to pull him out of the circle. Whoever succeeds in pulling him beyond the chalk line first will be declared the true mother."

Precious Pearl nodded to show she was willing to participate in the contest. Hai-tang was horrified.

"Begin," commanded Lord Bau.

Eagerly Precious Pearl clutched the little boy's wrist. Hai-tang wound her fingers lightly around Ping's other wrist. In the uneven contest, Precious Pearl yanked the boy out of the circle with ease. She beamed at her success and expected Lord Bau to award the child to her on the spot. Instead, she heard him direct a warning to Hai-tang.

"You did not follow my instructions. You did not pull hard enough. We will try once more. This time if you continue to

Ping's frightened cries filled the courtroom.

disobey me, your back will feel the smart of a bamboo rod." Lord Bau slammed his gavel on the table.

The judge observed both women closely. In contrast to Precious Pearl's tightened grip, Hai-tang barely touched Ping's wrist with her fingertips. Little Ping's frightened cries filled the courtroom.

"Enough," shouted Lord Bau. "Hai-tang, you have dared to disobey me a second time."

Hai-tang crumpled to the ground. Her entire body wracked with sobs, she beat her forehead against the hard floor.

"Your Excellency, I pray you to believe the child is mine. He is born of my flesh. I nursed him at my breast for three years. He is five years old and his bones are still fragile. If we both pull in opposite directions, he may be maimed for life. Rather would I give him up than cause him any harm."

"You, Hai-tang, are the true mother," declared Lord Bau, "for only a mother would put the well-being of her child before her own."

Jao, who had watched the whole spectacle unfold, sensed that the tide was turning against Precious Pearl. The truth was bound to come out, and he would certainly be implicated along with her. To save himself, or at least win a more lenient punishment, he volunteered to tell all. Precious Pearl's confession followed soon afterward. For the life she took, Precious Pearl forfeited her own. Because Jao had knowingly participated in Precious Pearl's wicked actions, his life was not spared either.

Jang Lin picked up his nephew and held him lovingly in his arms. He motioned to Hai-tang to follow him. For a long moment Hai-tang did not move. Now that her cruel ordeal was over she felt numb. Drained of all emotion, she hung her head and whispered a few words of gratitude to Lord Bau.

For the rest of her days Hai-tang's tranquil life was marred by only one regret. Her beloved husband, Officer Ma, had gone to his grave believing she was unfaithful.

A Stolen Stallion

Sying Fu considered himself a man graced by the benevolence of heaven. If the great one who reigns on high had not been moved by his pitiable plight, Sying Fu surely would have died, an unknown and unwanted waif on the streets of Kaifeng. Instead, he held the position of personal servant and companion to a wealthy merchant, a kind-hearted man who treated him like a son.

Never had Sying Fu forgotten the bitter days of his early childhood. Clothed in flimsy rags, shivering in the icy winds of winter, he was a mere beggar suffering from constant cold and hunger. One day, overcome by a wave of weakness, he had fainted and fallen to the ground. Vaguely he remembered being gently lifted and carried to a room where he was wrapped in a warm quilt and fed a bowl of life-restoring hot soup.

Master Du also believed that fate had intervened on his behalf by sending him to the rescue of the unfortunate child. Mourning the recent loss of his own six-year-old son, he had absentmindedly taken a wrong turn and found himself walking through a most disagreeable section of the city. The street teemed with beggars, gamblers, and thieves. The moment Master Du realized his mistake, he wanted to retrace his steps. But a hubbub of excited voices caught his attention. He edged his way toward a clump of people and found that they were clustered about the figure of a young boy who lay unmoving on the ground. Master Du's inquiries about the boy's identity met with blank faces. No

one knew who the ragged urchin was or from whence he had
come, only that he had collapsed suddenly and was feared dead.

Dropping to his knees, Master Du brought his ear close to the
child's breast. He heard the rhythmic beat of his heart and felt his
chest gently rise and fall with each breath. When Master Du
placed his hand on the little one's forehead, the boy opened his
eyes and stared bewildered at the strange face above him. Overcome with relief and pity, Master Du lifted the child in his arms.

"I will see to his needs," he announced to the onlookers, who
quickly dispersed, each going off on his own private errand. Thus
did Sying Fu become a part of Master Du's household.

Before Sying Fu reached his tenth birthday, Master Du realized his young charge did not possess a keen mind. However, his
cheerful obedience made up for the slowness of his wit. No
longer wanting for enough to eat, Sying Fu grew into a sturdy
youth. Frequently, Master Du's business activities took him far
from home and he formed the habit of taking Sying Fu along. His
amiable chatter chased away boredom and loneliness. Sying Fu
easily slipped into the position of a most favored servant.

When he was not traveling with his master, Sying Fu remained
at home charged with carrying out only the lightest and most
pleasant duties. He swept the pebbled walks, fed the goldfish in
the lily pond, trimmed the peonies and still had time to rest
leisurely on a garden bench enjoying the songs of warbling birds.
But the best part of every morning he spent at the three-sided
stable caring for Master Du's old mare.

He would lift the bar that held her safely in her stall and greet
her by running his hand lovingly over her face and neck. She
always responded by nuzzling him, expecting to be rewarded
with a handful of sweet grass. Sying Fu took pains to shovel the
manure into a neat pile and lay down fresh bedding before offering her grain and water. With a stiff brush he thoroughly cleaned
her coat until it was free of burrs and knots. This comfortable
daily routine suited Sying Fu's easy-going nature.

On a crisp, cool spring morning Sying Fu came to the stable as
usual to care for his friend. He was puzzled to find another horse

in her place. Puzzlement turned to wonder as he marveled at the unbelievably beautiful stallion.

The majestic animal measured fifteen hands high, his head erect and proud. With intelligent eyes he met Sying Fu's gaze, never once turning away. His dark brown coat glistened with good health, his black mane matched the fullness of his ebony tail. Sying Fu thought him the most majestic horse he had ever seen.

Slowly, he raised the bar. With easy movements and gentle whisperings, he stretched out his hand and patted the horse's rump. Hard muscles rippled under his fingers. Where, oh where did his master find such a noble stallion?

"I see you are admiring my new horse." Sying Fu turned around to find his master at his side. "Is he not a remarkable animal? I traded the old mare for him yesterday at the marketplace, and of course, I paid a handsome price. You must take good care of him, Sying Fu, for I treasure him as my prize possession."

"Have no fear," responded Sying Fu. "I too believe there is not another horse to match this one in all of China."

"Listen carefully," continued Master Du. "Tomorrow the rents on my properties are due and I must travel to Kaifeng. I intend to ride my new stallion to the home of my friend, Master Li, and go on foot from there. You have accompanied me to his house many times and should have no trouble finding your way through the city. Meet me there at noon. If you start walking as soon as I leave, you will arrive with time to spare. You are to take charge of the stallion and lead him back home. I have many affairs to attend to in the city. I shall return late in the evening in a hired sedan chair."

Sying Fu was awake the next morning earlier than usual. In preparation for his master's journey, he fed the stallion, put fresh water in his pail, and groomed him vigorously. After combing the horse's tail, he held it aside to brush his rump. It was then that he noticed a white circular mark on the left flank, an unusual spot of color on the otherwise uniformly brown hide.

Master Du, ready to leave on the day's errands, came to the stable where he found Sying Fu examining the stallion's mouth.

"Are all the horse's teeth there or are you looking for some hidden treasure?" Sying Fu ignored the good-humored teasing.

"Master, one cusp on the last tooth of the right upper jaw has broken off."

"Don't concern yourself about that. Such an imperfection will neither be seen nor will it decrease the stallion's appetite. You are almost too thorough, Sying Fu."

His master's amiable mood prompted Sying Fu to ask a favor.

"Sir, would you permit me to ride the horse home from Master Li's house? It is a long, wearying walk. Sying Fu's voice quivered with excitement. Master Du shook his head. The idea did not please him, but Sying Fu appeared so crestfallen the older man changed his mind.

"Very well," he agreed, "be sure to keep a slow, steady pace and take him directly to his stall. I shall hold you responsible should any harm come to him." Master Du swung himself up on the horse's gleaming back.

"See that you get to Master Li's house by noon," he reminded Sying Fu before riding off.

Sying Fu hastened to prepare himself for the day's outing. He gulped down a meager breakfast, changed his shirt, and set out, striding briskly toward the city. Rarely did he have an opportunity to go anywhere unaccompanied. With time to spare, he anticipated having the freedom to wander leisurely through the streets of Kaifeng.

Kaifeng was a cosmopolitan metropolis, criss-crossed by flowing streams and canals. It teemed with people. Sying Fu enjoyed strolling at will, peeking into narrow alleyways, stopping at the numerous stalls where silks and porcelains were sold. Best of all, he was fascinated by the many unusual tradesmen, dressed in exotic outfits from distant places he could never hope to visit.

In good time, Sying Fu arrived at Master Li's house. Master Du was pleased by his promptness. He impressed upon his servant once again that he was being entrusted with the valuable stallion, that he was to take him directly back to the stable without stopping for any reason. Smugly anticipating the envious glances of all who would pass him on the road, the eager Sying

Fu mounted the horse, grasped the reins, and rode out of Master Li's yard.

Now the trustworthy and dependable Sying Fu had every intention of following his master's instructions. Were it not that the rains had been delayed, that the road was extremely dusty, that his mouth felt dry, he would not have stopped at a shaded pavilion where a large earthen jug filled with cool tea had been set out for the convenience of thirsty travelers. He welcomed the opportunity to soothe his scratchy throat. First he tied the horse securely to a pavilion post. Then he dipped the wooden ladle into the jug and served himself a refreshing drink. He was about to resume his journey when a well-dressed man leading a grey mule hailed him.

"Young brother, I hope you will pardon me for detaining you, but I can't help admiring your wonderful horse." Sying Fu thrust out his chest, delighted to be taken for the stallion's owner.

"Rarely have I seen a grander looking steed," remarked the stranger, circling the horse and examining him from every angle. "Where did you get him?"

"I bought him from a horse trader." Sying Fu was not beyond bending the truth a bit.

"Why I, too, make my living buying and selling horses. My name is Hwang Hung," the stranger offered by way of introducing himself. "You are very lucky to own such a valuable animal. Would you perhaps consider selling him to me?"

"Oh no! I would never part with him."

"I understand the way you feel," said Hwang Hung. "What a delight it must be to ride him."

Sying Fu was anxious to leave. He was finding the man tiresome. He started to untie the horse from the post but the stranger detained him.

"Pardon me if I make so bold as to ask a favor. I have never ridden such a splendid horse. Would you just allow me to take him for a slow walk here in front of the pavilion? I truly envy you for you can ride him at your pleasure every day."

Of a naive and guileless nature, Sying Fu permitted himself to be swayed. "Only for a little while," he agreed, handing the reins to the stranger. To himself he reasoned, "It will be just one turn around the pavilion and Master Du need never know about it."

Hwang Hung mounted the stallion. True to his promise he began to walk him slowly around the pavilion. The next minute he had spurred him to a trot, circling the pavilion again and again. Sying Fu began to feel uneasy and signaled Hwang Hung to dismount. Instead, Hwang Hung dug his knees into the stallion's ribs, slapped him on the rump, and with a shrill cry took off at a wild gallop. Sying Fu, his mouth agape, his eyes blurred by a whirlwind of dust, gazed in horror at the fast-disappearing rider.

"Gone, gone! How could I have been so foolish?" cried Sying Fu, grasping his head between his hands. He stood rooted to the spot, bemoaning the calamity that had overtaken him.

The braying of Hwang Hung's mule brought him back to his senses. Reality dawned on him. He had been tricked. Hwang Hung had stolen his master's magnificent stallion and left a scrawny, sway-backed mule in his place. Perspiration gathered at Sying Fu's temples. "What shall I tell Master? Oh what curses and blows will rain down upon my head!"

The despondent Sying Fu rode the mule back home and secured her in the stable. Foregoing his supper, he went immediately to the servants' quarters. He fell upon his mat, curled his body into a ball, and shut his eyes. His mind continued to conjure up Master Du's fury.

Although it was almost dark when Master Du returned from Kaifeng, he stopped first to look in at his stallion. The sight of the old mule in the stallion's stall alarmed him. Suspecting that something dreadful had happened to his horse, he rushed to the servants' quarters to find Sying Fu. He grabbed his servant by the hair and yanked him to his feet.

"Where is my stallion? What have you done with him?" he demanded.

"Master, I am sorry, forgive me," blubbered Sying Fu.

Master Du's face flushed with rage.

"Where is he? Where is my horse?" he screamed.

Hwang Hung dug his knees into the stallion's ribs
and took off at a wild gallop.

Panic-stricken, Sying Fu's throat tightened. Not a word could he utter.

"Speak, you blockhead, speak!"

His teeth chattering, Sying Fu managed to recount the afternoon's events.

Amid curses and threats, Master Du slapped Sying Fu again and again.

"Sniveling fool, how could you let a perfect stranger ride my horse? Oh, why did I save you years ago? It would have been better to let you perish in the street." The beating and yelling finally tired Master Du. He let his hands drop to his sides.

"I do not wish to set eyes upon you again," he exclaimed bitterly. "Leave at once!"

Sying Fu threw himself on the ground. He hugged Master Du's ankles, pleading for forgiveness.

"I promise I shall find him," he whimpered. "I shall bring back your horse, only do not send me away. Where can I go? I have no other home but here."

Master Du was unforgiving of Sying Fu's stupidity, but, at the same time, he was not unmoved by Sying Fu's pleas. The face of the poor homeless child he once rescued from starvation flashed before him. He relented. "I will give you ten days to have the stallion back in the stable. If you do not find him within that time, you will be out on the streets of the city, begging for a mouthful of food." Master Du kicked his legs free of Sying Fu's arms and left.

That night, Sying Fu caught not a wink of sleep. How could he possibly locate Hwang Hung? His head swam with a jumble of impractical ideas. He decided to start his search in Kaifeng. For three days he combed the city's streets, seeking information about the whereabouts of the horse trader. No one he asked had ever heard of a person named Hwang Hung. Sying Fu surrendered to panic.

On the fourth day Sying Fu was wandering aimlessly along a deserted street. A wrinkled old woman, her back bent with the weight of a bundle of sticks, shuffled toward him.

"May I help you with your load, auntie?" Sying Fu inquired. She was so frail she seemed at the point of collapse. The woman allowed Sying Fu to relieve her of the heavy burden.

"I do not recognize you," she remarked, peering into Sying Fu's face. "You are not from these parts."

Sying Fu explained why he had come to Kaifeng. Like all others from whom he had inquired about Hwang Hung, she, too, denied knowing anyone by that name.

"Do not waste your time on a futile search," the old woman advised. "Take your problem to Lord Bau." She spoke no more until they reached the street where she lived. She thanked Sying Fu, retrieved her bundle, and disappeared behind a weatherbeaten door.

Taking to heart the old woman's counsel, Sying Fu appeared at the *yamen*. It was now the fifth day of his search for Hwang Hung. A slight stirring of hope rose in Sying Fu's breast only to be dashed when he was told that Lord Bau was unable to see him until the following morning. Precious time was slipping by and nothing had been accomplished.

On the sixth day Sying Fu entered the imposing government building. He was asked to wait until Lord Bau was ready to see him. In his state of anxiety he could feel his heart pounding against his chest. At last he was ushered into the judge's presence and told to state his case.

In setting forth his complaint against Hwang Hung, Sying Fu did not shrink from blaming himself for his vanity, his boasting, his poor judgment, but, "After all," he added in self-defense, "it is Hwang Hung, not I, who is the horse thief. To tell a little lie is not as grave an offense as stealing a horse."

Lord Bau quickly made it plain that he was not interested in Sying Fu's opinions. "I will be the judge as to the seriousness of the crime, if a crime was indeed committed."

The reprimand took Sying Fu by surprise. His confidence was further shaken by the direction Lord Bau's questioning took. "Are you accusing this Hwang Hung of being a horse thief to cover up your own disobedience to your master? Can you positively identify the stallion you claim was stolen? What proof can you offer?"

"I am truly lost," thought Sying Fu. Fear tied his tongue. He remained mute. Then he remembered the white mark on the horse's rump. His tongue came unstuck and he smiled. "Honorable Lord, I will know my master's stallion as soon as I set eyes upon him. What's more, I have but to lift his tail to expose an unusual marking, a small white spot, as round as the character for the sun." Sying Fu was sure he saw Lord Bau raise his eyebrows. Sying Fu took heart. "There is yet another way to identify Master Du's stallion. He has one imperfect tooth. On the upper jaw, the last tooth on the right side has a cusp missing."

"Very well," said Lord Bau, satisfied that Sying Fu was telling the truth. "It may be possible to locate the thief and retrieve the stallion, but it will not be done easily. Unless you can be depended upon to follow orders, we will fail. You did not obey your master and brought all this trouble down upon yourself," Lord Bau reminded him.

"I give you my solemn oath that I will do exactly as you command. Please, Honorable Lord," Sying Fu pleaded, "anything, anything you direct me to do I will gladly do, only help me find Master Du's stallion."

"Then heed what I am about to say. For the next two days you must refrain from feeding Hwang Hung's mule. No matter how loudly she brays, give her nothing but water. On the third morning, one hour after sunrise, you are to bring the mule to the courtyard of the *yamen*. There, Officer Chang will await you. Whatever he asks of you, obey to the letter. Remember, do not let the mule eat even a single blade of grass."

Sying Fu returned home feeling more desolate than ever. How could a starving mule bring back a missing horse? Worse still, the ninth day of his hunt for Hwang Hung will have begun by the time he was to meet with Officer Chang.

A mule deprived of sustenance protests loudly. The warmhearted Sying Fu found the mule's incessant braying pitiful. More than once he was sorely tempted to give her a ration of grain but held back. Instead, he tried to soothe her, patting her flank, murmuring in her ear, offering yet another pail of water. She only cried the louder, thrashing about in her stall. Exhausted, she fell silent, only to rest for a while before starting the ruckus all over again.

Sying Fu's considerable skills in caring for animals were stretched to the limit. He had to figure out a way to walk the mule to the *yamen* and keep her from stopping to munch on the grass along the way. After much head-scratching, he hit on a novel solution. From a nearby swamp, he gathered reeds and wove them expertly into a basket. On the day he was to appear at the *yamen*, he fit the basket over the mule's mouth and secured it behind her big ears with strong string. He was about to climb atop her back when she sank down, stretched her forelegs stiffly in front of her, and refused to budge. Sying Fu tugged at the rope he had placed around her neck, shouted and cajoled, to no avail. The stubborn mule, weakened from lack of food, would not rise. In a last desperate attempt to get her moving, Sying Fu held a handful of grass in front of her nose and raised it high in the air. As she bounded to her feet, Sying Fu hoisted himself onto the mule's back, delivered a hard kick to her sides and they were off at last.

The going was anything but smooth. Wild grasses growing by the side of the road were a constant temptation to the hungry mule. She struggled to rid herself of the basket and balked at every step.

Sying Fu was worn out by the time he arrived at the courtyard of the *yamen*. Officer Chang, seated on a strong horse, was waiting for him. The peculiar muzzle affixed to the mule's ears brought an amused smile to Officer Chang's face. He complimented Sying Fu for devising such an ingenious contraption.

"Now we must proceed at once," he said, turning serious. "You are to take the mule back to the pavilion where you first encountered Hwang Hung. There she may pick up a familiar scent. With her nose to guide her, and with luck, she will lead us to the man who stole Master Du's stallion."

Sying Fu did not place much faith in the mule. His doubts seemed justified, for as soon as they reached the pavilion and secured the mule to a stake, the pathetic animal's legs buckled and she rolled over on her side. Sying Fu was concerned lest she die. But her breathing, though shallow, was steady. Helplessly he watched for some sign of recovery. The mule remained motionless.

By afternoon the sky had become overcast, and in the distance, Sying Fu heard the rumbling of thunder. Dark, heavy-laden clouds blew in, propelled by a stiff breeze. The mule lifted her head and sniffed the air. Her nostrils flared in and out, her upper lip retracted, exposing her protruding teeth and pink gums. Suddenly, she was up on her feet, tugging wildly at the restraining rope. The stake came free. She startled Officer Chang and Sying Fu with a high-pitched whinny before dashing directly into the wind, galloping as fast as her clumsy body would permit.

"Climb on," yelled Officer Chang, who, in one flowing movement, heaved himself onto his horse. Sying Fu jumped up behind him.

From then on, the mule led them on a chase, turning and twisting down narrow roads, cutting across ripening grain fields, hurtling over low fences until they reached Yellow Earth Village. There she found a lane leading to a thatched cottage. Officer Chang and Sying Fu dismounted and followed the panting mule across a stone bridge into a small yard. Sying Fu tied her to a tree stump and removed the muzzle. The grateful animal immediately began to crop the sparse grass near her.

Officer Chang pounded on the cottage door. There was no reply. He kicked the door open. With Sying Fu following at his heels, he walked through the two-room dwelling. Unwashed cooking pans and a table strewn with dirty bowls made him wonder whether the place was deserted. Officer Chang and Sying Fu next explored the outside of the house. Cautiously they crept around toward the back. In a makeshift corral, fifty paces beyond the cottage, they saw a man currying a tall stallion.

"There he is," shouted Sying Fu. "There is Master Du's stallion, and there is the vile swindler who stole him." Delirious with excitement, Sying Fu ran toward the horse, but the man stepped in front of him and restrained him.

"By what right do you come uninvited to hurl false accusations at me? And who is your companion? Remove yourselves at once, or I will throw you off my property."

Officer Chang ignored Hwang Hung's attempt to scare them

Officer Chang and Sying Fu followed the mule
as she ran toward a thatched cottage.

off. He identified himself as an aide to Lord Bau and informed
Hwang Hung that he was under arrest. His mission, he explained,
was not to determine who was truthful and who was lying. Lord
Bau was the one to make that judgment. With an air of authority he
added, "Now both of you will accompany me to Kaifeng. Sying Fu,
you ride the horse; Hwang Hung, you follow on the mule."

All the way from Yellow Earth Village to the capital, worry
weighed heavily on Hwang Hung. Fearing the consequences of his
crime, he tried desperately to think of some plausible alibi. But
what if the judge were not as easy to outwit as the gullible Sying
Fu? Hwang Hung did not dwell for long on that possibility. Possessed of an over-blown arrogance, he considered himself a match
for any man.

Just as daylight was fading, Sying Fu, Hwang Hung and Officer Chang entered the *yamen* gate. Lord Bau had already retired
to his living quarters and would hear no more cases that day.
Sying Fu and Hwang Hung spent a troubled night in a common
cell. They actually felt a sense of relief when the guard summoned them and escorted them to the courtroom.

On their knees, their foreheads touching the floor, both were
tense with anxiety. The one fretted that the ten-day period of grace
was about to end, the other that his guilt would be unmasked.

"You stand accused of stealing Master Du's precious stallion."
Hwang Hung was jolted by Lord Bau's severe tone but quickly
regained his composure.

"No, Most Honorable Judge, the horse belongs to me. I bought
him from a farmer two weeks ago."

"Did you examine the horse thoroughly before you purchased
him?" inquired Lord Bau. "Does he have any special features,
marks of identity which are peculiar to him alone? Did you inspect his coat? Did you look in his mouth?"

To each question Hwang Hung replied with confidence, adding that he had bought and sold many a horse.

"It was absurd to think I would consider one that was less than
perfect," he boldly declared. "This one's hide was shiny brown
from head to tail; his every tooth was sound."

Lord Bau addressed Sying Fu.

"Does the description of the horse as given by Hwang Hung fit Master Du's stallion?"

"It is not so, Honorable Sir. My master's horse is truly a fine animal, but he is not without a flaw."

"Then let the animal be brought into the courtroom."

Under the watchful eye of a guard, Hwang Hung was directed to lift the horse's tail. The round white mark stood out clearly. Next, Sying Fu was ordered to pry open the horse's mouth and point out the broken tooth. Hwang Hung had to confirm that the last tooth on the right upper jaw was missing a cusp.

Lord Bau confronted Hwang Hung. "This horse does not appear to be the perfect specimen, free of all blemishes, that you described."

Hwang Hung's self-assurance melted away. In an almost inaudible voice he admitted his shameless misdeed.

Lord Bau pronounced the sentence. "Each day, from sunup to sundown, for a full month, Hwang Hung is to be paraded through his village with a large paper sign suspended from his neck bearing the inscription HORSE THIEF. He will be required to pass through every street and every lane and never be permitted to rest. If he falters, the jailers at his side will prod him to move on in the same way one coaxes a horse, with the lash of a whip. Hwang Hung's humiliation will serve as a warning to others tempted to acquire by trickery that which is not theirs."

On his way home astride the stallion, Sying Fu again came to the pavilion. The prospect of a rest in the shade and a sip of cool tea beckoned him. His first impulse was to stop, but he rode on. This was the place where he had earlier come to grief. He resolved not to chance being led into another misadventure. Before sunset of the tenth day he would have the stallion safely in the stable. Despite his past blunders Master Du would forgive him. Sying Fu breathed freely. Fortune had favored him yet another time.

The Stone Lion

Although the residents of the village of Shrtou in the county of Deng knew that far to the north the earth sometimes shook, and that, with the melting of the snows, the Yellow River often went on a rampage, they were not concerned. The prosperous inhabitants believed they had been blessed by heaven. A benevolent stream meandered peacefully through their fertile land, providing them with a steady supply of fresh water, and the stable earth with its dark rich loam assured them of bountiful harvests. Each night, wrapped in warm quilts, they slept soundly, certain they would awake the next morning to another peaceful day.

Yet, in time, the happiness that should have been their lot turned sour. From among the many, a few men, driven by greed, amassed great wealth at the expense of their neighbors. They built fine houses, dressed in costly garments, and were carried about the village in richly decorated sedan chairs.

Flaunting their worldly possessions before their less fortunate neighbors, they spread seeds of dissatisfaction. Greed crept into the hearts of formerly virtuous and honorable men. Jealousy led to quarrels; seething hostility erupted into violence. Within the family, wives lost respect for their husbands, and children no longer obeyed their parents. The strict Confucian code that for centuries had governed daily existence was forgotten.

A dark cloud descended over the land.

There remained in this unhappy village but one family whose

members clung faithfully to the great sage's tenets. Within the walls of their home all was harmonious. The head of the household, Master Tswei Ching, found no fault with his gentle wife, Ming. Both doted on their only son, Wen, who, in return, was dearly devoted to his parents.

Master Tswei Ching was a man of ample means, having earned his money by honest labor. And he was also a most generous man. Every summer he had his cook prepare large jugs of tea to set out at the roadside. A tired traveler could slake his thirst by ladling out a bowl of life-restoring brew. During the winter, many a starving vagrant came to Tswei Ching's gate for a serving of hot rice gruel prepared fresh twice each day. If ever a grieving family found itself without enough money to bury a dead relative, Tswei Ching was ready to extend a helping hand. Nor did he overlook the poor elderly folk. They were provided with healing herbs at his expense.

Tswei Ching's benevolence did not endear him to his neighbors. They were a rough lot given to quarreling. Their coarse language was an embarrassment. As for showing consideration for others, they were the opposite of Tswei Ching. They lived by a different set of rules.

Close to the peak of Wutai Mountain, a short distance from the village of Shrtou, stood an ancient temple. There, a sect of religious monks who worshipped the great Buddha intoned their unceasing prayers. Among them dwelt one whose extraordinary piety commanded the utmost respect from the others. Although his body had withered with age, his religious fervor had not abated. On occasion, the holy man took it upon himself to venture forth into the village of Shrtou, seeking donations for the upkeep of the temple. It was a difficult undertaking for one so frail, but it was made even more disheartening by the reception he received from the villagers. At almost every door he was turned away with not so much as an offer of a bowl of tea or a place to sit and rest for a while. Only at the home of Tswei Ching did he find a warm welcome as an honored guest. Respectful of the monk's advanced years, every member of the family and the servants, as well, paid him homage. When it came time to take his leave, he would express his grateful appreciation, and Tswei Ching would press several pieces of silver into his hand before bidding him farewell.

A lifetime of devotion and prayer had earned the monk special recognition among the immortals. He was given the power to foresee the future. Thus it was that he knew beforehand of the catastrophe about to befall the village of Shrtou. On one of his rare descents from Wutai Mountain, he disclosed to Tswei Ching a dire prediction.

"The Emperor of Heaven," he confided, "has become sorely vexed by the inhabitants of Shrtou. For many years they have tried his patience, but he has held back his wrath, hoping they would mend their ways. He can no longer abide their wickedness. With the coming of spring, he will send a great flood to sweep them all from the face of the earth." The monk stopped to catch his breath. He saw the look of horror in Tswei Ching's eyes and hastened to reassure him.

"But the merciful Emperor of Heaven will never permit a worthy man to suffer. Therefore, Tswei Ching, you and your household are destined to be saved. Make ready for the deluge by building a stout junk large enough to carry your family, your servants, your farm animals. When the river swells and turns the village into a vast lake, your junk will sail high and dry, safe from danger.

"Now harken to what I am about to say. Should a bird seek refuge upon the deck of your junk, do not drive it away. Should an animal be seen floundering in the water, go to its rescue. But if a human being cries out for help, you must, without exception, ignore the plea."

The enormity of the foreordained calamity was beyond Tswei Ching's ability to imagine.

"But, Venerable Sage," he asked, regaining his composure, "will there be any sign to warn me of the imminence of the flood, a signal that will tell me it is time to board the junk?"

"Indeed, my master," whispered the monk. "It has all been arranged. Upon carved pedestals at either side of the village gate sit two stone lions. Do not concern yourself with the one on the right. But when the eyes of the lion on the left shed tears of blood, you must make final preparations."

Tswei Ching gathered his family and servants to tell them of the monk's frightful warning. They listened to him with disbelief.

"We cannot argue against the decree of the Emperor of Heaven. He will protect us from harm," he said, attempting to allay their fears.

Tswei Ching set about making plans for the construction of a large junk. He ordered the skilled carpenters among his servants to gather the necessary materials and begin work without delay.

Mindful of the monk's instructions, Tswei Ching sent one of his maids to inspect the statue every day precisely at noon. He instructed her to look closely into the lion's eyes.

"If you find one eye red with blood, do not tarry, but return home at once."

And so, each day at the appointed time, the maid appeared in front of the stone lion. Standing on tiptoe, she would peer into the statue's eyes, nod her head slightly as if satisfied with what she saw, retrace her steps and report to her master.

The maid's seemingly strange behavior aroused the curiosity of the village butcher whose shop was nearby. Once he approached her and questioned her directly.

"What do you see there? What do you expect to find in the blank eyes of a stone statue?"

The untutored girl answered innocently.

"When blood flows from the eyes of the lion, there will come a great flood. So tells my master."

The butcher sniggered at her foolishness. He found her story so ludicrous he passed it on to everyone he met. Tswei Ching became the butt of ribald jokes and ridicule.

Not content to let the matter rest, the butcher was bent on some playful mischief. The next time he slaughtered a pig, he saved a bowl of the animal's blood. Just before Tswei Ching's maid arrived for her daily inspection, he smeared an eye of the statue to the left of the gate with the sticky fluid. Standing in the doorway of his shop, he watched the maid approach. As was her custom, she mounted the pedestal to make her usual inspection.

But this time she did not nod her head. Instead, she jumped backward in such haste she almost lost her balance.

"It has happened! Tears of blood, tears of blood," she screamed as she dashed for home.

The butcher burst into gales of laughter. What a clever trick he had played on Tswei Ching! He couldn't wait to spread the news through the village.

The maid's report sent Tswei Ching's household into a flurry of activity. The master urged his carpenters to complete the building of the junk as quickly as possible. He ordered all the other servants to assist in every way, preparing food, carting materials, keeping the lanterns burning so that work could continue uninterrupted after dusk. The final touches were still incomplete when Tswei Ching gave the command to board the junk. The deck was a jumble of people, grunting pigs and clucking chickens, baskets overflowing with rice, jugs of water, warm quilts and rolls of sleeping mats. Everyone was filled with foreboding, uncertain of what lay ahead.

For three days a blazing sun continued to hang overhead. Every night stars twinkled in the cloudless, velvet sky. Jammed together in close quarters, beset by heat and unpleasant smells, grumblings of discontent were soon heard among the fainthearted. Tswei Ching, himself, began to wonder whether he had permitted himself to fall victim to a colossal hoax. Yet he ordered everyone to remain on board.

At dawn of the fourth morning, Tswei Ching stood on deck scanning the horizon. Everyone was becoming increasingly restless. Though no one dared say it aloud, he sensed they were blaming him for their discomfort. He decided to wait through this one day. If there were no sign of an imminent flood, he would give the order to disembark.

Of course, Tswei Ching did not know that many *li*[*] to the west the swollen Yellow River was already spreading havoc in all directions.

Wen, who was also on deck facing in the direction of Shrtou's

---

[*]Chinese unit of distance, equal to approximately 1/3 mile.

once peaceful stream, suddenly cried out, "A wall of water is coming this way." Within seconds a foaming torrent of swirling eddies crashed against the junk. All on board felt themselves being lifted off the solid earth. Fearing for their lives, they huddled together and beseeched heaven for mercy.

By the following morning, the worst was over. The junk floated smoothly, a tiny speck in an immense, calm sea. Uprooted trees, bits of household furnishings, carcasses of drowned animals, and, worst of all, bloated human bodies bobbing in the water gave evidence of the terrible punishment that had been wreaked upon the people of Shrtou. One by one, the servants bowed before Tswei Ching, thanking him for saving their lives.

"It is not I who deserves your gratitude," responded their master. "We have survived by the grace of the mighty one who rules heaven and earth."

The loud cawing of a crow suddenly pierced the air. Looking for a place to rest, the bird circled the junk hopefully. Tswei Ching told Wen to set out a small bowl of grain. For a short while, the bird continued to circle cautiously overhead. With its black wings outspread, it glided down, alighting near the bowl. Greedily it pecked at the food, then found a comfortable perch near the back of the junk, where it settled down to rest.

It was just before sunset that a monkey was sighted clinging to a board in the muddy waters. Tswei Ching extended a long pole toward the terrified animal. Hand over hand the monkey climbed up the pole until he reached the safety of the deck. He shook himself, loosening a spray of droplets before jumping onto a barrel. There he sat, waiting for his fur to dry.

The day was fading quickly. The rays of the sinking sun painted the western sky in bands of red and orange. But for the lapping of the water along the sides of the junk, all was quiet. A faint cry reached Wen's sharp ears first.

"Someone is calling for help," he shouted. There was a rush to the railing. Looking in the direction of Wen's pointed finger, a man could be seen floundering in the water.

"Save me, save me!" came a desperate cry for help.

"Save me, save me!" came a desperate cry for help.

The old monk's admonition rang clearly in Tswei Ching's head. "If you save a single human being you will bring misfortune down upon yourself."

The cry became fainter. Time was running out for the exhausted swimmer. In an instant he could slip out of sight forever. Tswei Ching's kind heart would not allow him to stand idly by and watch a kindred soul perish. He ordered one of his servants to throw a rope to the struggling swimmer. The half-dead fellow was hauled up on board. Shivering in the cool air and coughing to clear his water-clogged lungs, he moved everyone to pity. He seemed to be no more than a year or two older than Wen. Tswei Ching held off questioning him until he had changed into dry clothes and had finished a bowl of hot broth.

"I am Liu Ying, son of the butcher," he offered in answer to Tswei Ching's kind queries. "I was helping my father in his shop when a sudden roaring noise frightened me. In a flash, we were swept away by an overpowering rush of water. I was fighting for my last breath when you so mercifully plucked me from certain death." Out of immediate peril, Liu Ying realized the enormity of his losses.

"My parents are surely drowned," he sobbed. "I am without a home, an orphan adrift in a shattered world."

Tswei Ching was touched by the young man's misery.

"You need not despair," he comforted. "We shall gladly welcome you into our family and cherish you as a true son."

The grateful Liu Ying made a solemn promise.

"Some day I shall repay you a hundredfold for the goodness you have shown me."

It was not long after Liu Ying's rescue that the waters began to recede. The sun rose high in the sky and sent its warm rays to dry up the sodden land. When at last all danger had passed, those on board Tswei Ching's junk were able to disembark. How thankful they were to set foot on dry land once again.

An eerie silence pervaded the atmosphere. Reminders of human habitation were strewn about everywhere. Only a few battered houses remained standing; among them, Tswei Ching's. By some miracle the stone lions that had flanked the city gates were intact, still resting upon their pedestals. But they had nothing to guard save emptiness.

The task of rebuilding Tswei Ching's house took many weeks. Gradually the household settled down into its former routines. Never more did the crow venture far afield. She learned to respond to Wen's whistle, coming to perch upon his shoulder at his call. The monkey, too, found a niche within the family, following at Wen's heels wherever he went. A strong bond of affection grew between them. Liu Ying was more than content to be a son to Tswei Ching and a brother to Wen.

With the passing of time, people from far away regions wandered into the fertile valley. The village of Shrtou was restored and thrived anew.

On a day when his chores were lighter than usual, Tswei Ching was enjoying a restful hour in the tea house among friends. There he first overheard talk of the Queen Mother's jade seal. It had vanished without a trace. Though the palace was searched from end to end, the seal had not been found. The emperor was offering to reward the person who could locate it with a high position in the government.

"Someone may be lucky," chuckled Tswei Ching to himself, dismissing the thought that it was any concern of his.

That night he slept soundly but awoke before the blackness in his room had turned to grey. It was too early to rise, so he lay in bed, eyes closed. Soothed by the first chirping of the sparrows, he dropped off again into a sound sleep. In a vivid dream, an old shrunken holy man with a shaved head appeared at his side. In his hand he carried a horsehair flail. Shaking it gently he delivered his message in a husky, grating voice.

"The Queen Mother's seal lies at the bottom of an abandoned dry well behind the palace."

Tswei Ching sat up with a start. The dawn's dim light had already begun to dispel the darkness from the eastern sky. He climbed off the *kang* and began to pull on his clothes. His moving about caused his wife to stir. Half awake, Ming asked sleepily,

"Is something amiss?"

"No," Tswei Ching assured her. "It's just that I had the strangest dream. An ancient holy man spoke to me. His head had not a single hair upon it. His face was grey, the color of death. So thin and shrunken was he, I was sure he had returned from his tomb beyond the yellow springs. In a broken, husky voice he revealed to me the location of the Queen Mother's lost seal."

"Surely it is a sign from heaven," declared Ming, nodding her head vigorously. "We must not make light of it. What do you plan to do?"

Tswei Ching shook his head. "Perhaps I should do nothing."

"No, no," cried Ming. "If a holy man appears in a dream to deliver an urgent message, you must not ignore it."

"Very well, then, I shall ask Wen to go to the capital. If he can recover the lost seal, he will reap the reward. We shall be so proud of him when he becomes a court official."

"That we must not do," came Ming's worried reply. "I fear he may meet with some mishap if we send him so far away from home."

Later in the day, the matter was discussed among all the family members. Liu Ying, realizing Ming's concern for her own son, offered to go in Wen's place.

"It is the least I can do in return for your kindness to me. If I succeed in finding the seal and receive a large sum of money as a reward, I shall share it with my brother. Should I be offered an official appointment, I shall humbly decline and propose that, instead, the honor be bestowed upon Wen." Thus it was agreed that Liu Ying would journey to Kaifeng.

After the necessary preparations were completed, Liu Ying took leave of his father, mother and brother.

"Never will I forget my family," he solemnly promised.

Upon his arrival in the city, Liu Ying went directly to the royal palace. A court eunuch, softened by a bribe, agreed to arrange an appearance before the emperor. Liu Ying was overwhelmed by the magnificence of the throne room and the splendor of the furnishings. When the emperor entered, Liu Ying dared not look

at his face. On his knees, head bent forward almost touching the
floor, he could see only the hem of the emperor's embroidered
robes. With great pomp and ceremony, the emperor was seated,
and his attendants, bowing from the waist, backed away to take
up their customary positions. Liu Ying humbly petitioned the
emperor to allow him to search for the Queen Mother's lost seal,
adding that he had good reason to believe it was to be found in
the well behind the palace.

The emperor regarded Liu Ying with suspicion.

"There have been many who have come before you. Each one
claimed he knew exactly where the seal lay. Each failed in his
attempt to locate it. I am grown tired of the parade of fools.
Unless you can convince me that you know whereof you speak, I
shall dismiss you forthwith."

Eager to reassure the skeptical monarch, Liu Ying concocted
the lie that the ruler of Heaven himself had appeared to him and
disclosed the location of the seal. The smooth-tongued man succeeded in swaying the emperor, who granted him permission to
proceed.

With the aid of several palace eunuchs, Liu Ying was lowered
into the depths of the well. Just as predicted in Tswei Ching's
dream, the seal lay on the pebbly bottom. Without difficulty, Liu
Ying recovered the precious object. Amidst much rejoicing, the
jade seal was returned to the Queen Mother.

For his effort, the emperor appointed Liu Ying his chief
court advisor. In a position of newly acquired power, Liu Ying
conveniently forgot all the promises he had made to his family.

At home in Shrtou, Tswei Ching was anxiously awaiting news
from Kaifeng. When, after several months, no messenger had
arrived, he became concerned. Word finally came by way of a
traveling merchant who was passing through the village. He let it
be known that the Queen Mother's jade seal had been found by a
young man from the village of Shrtou who goes by the name of
Liu Ying.

At first, Tswei Ching felt reassured that nothing untoward had
happened to his adopted son, but with the continued absence of addi-

tional news, he became apprehensive. He could not rest until he knew for certain why there was no further word from Liu Ying. Despite Ming's protestations, he resolved to send Wen to the capital.

"You must find your brother," he instructed. "Only by talking directly to him will we learn why he has not broken his silence. I cannot believe that he would fail to keep his solemn pledge."

Wen did not leave home unaccompanied. The monkey skipped jauntily beside him, while the crow sat upon his shoulder, cawing loudly. Behind them walked a servant carrying provisions for the journey. Wen and his companions reached the city gates without misfortune. The odd group of travelers attracted the attention of all who passed them by.

A sudden clattering of hoofs sent people scurrying. They made way for a well-groomed official sitting stiffly on a chestnut stallion. Wen recognized his brother at once. Eagerly he pushed his way toward the mounted rider, calling out, "Liu Ying, my brother, how happy I am to find you!"

Liu Ying paled at the sight of Wen, for he had already wiped away all memory of his former family and wanted no reminder. He reined in his horse. Pretending not to know the young man who had called to him, he shouted haughtily, "How dare you address me so familiarly? I know you not. Seize this impudent ruffian," he ordered his guards. "Give him a few lashes to teach him proper respect for his betters, and throw him into jail!"

Terrified that Liu Ying would turn his wrath on him as well, the good servant swiftly disappeared into the milling throng. The monkey clambered atop a shed, out of harm's way, while the crow circled above the scene, screeching nervously. Liu Ying spurred his horse and rode off. He congratulated himself on the ease with which he had rid himself of a threat to his exalted position. Surely, Wen would not last very long under the harsh prison conditions.

Sore and bloodied, Wen lay on the damp jail floor, his bruised back a constant reminder of his brother's perfidy. Were it not for the dim light filtering through a small, barred opening near the top of the outside wall, Wen would not have known night from day. His jailors never spoke to him. Once in a while, a bowl of slimy soup was shoved under the door. Many times, Wen did not touch it, so revolted was he by its smell. Ever hungry and constantly cold, his health deteriorated rapidly. In his hopelessness and despair he often wished for the release of death.

One morning, Wen arose shaking from the bone-chilling dankness. Not yet fully awake, he became aware of an odd scratching sound. Surely his eyes must be deceiving him, for poking through the small, barred opening was a monkey's arm. The furry paw held a round, red plum. Starved as he was, Wen lunged for it, afraid it would disappear. Not for a long time had he tasted anything so delicious.

Thereafter Wen's old friend brought whatever nourishment he could find for his master. He pulled fruits off tree branches, gathered berries, stole vegetables ripening in private gardens. Gradually Wen regained his strength and the monkey's continuing visits buoyed his spirits.

Wen's hopes were further restored when he was roused a few days later by the cawing of a crow. He caught a glimpse of the bird's black shape each time she flew past the opening at the top of the wall. When he whistled to her, she came to rest, clinging to a bar with one foot and poking her other foot through the opening. Wen knew she was his own feathered friend. He took the bird's curious behavior as a signal that she, too, had come to help him. Of course, she could carry a message to his father!

Wen ripped a small piece of cloth from the end of his shirt. Unmindful of pain, he bit into his index finger until it bled. Using his bleeding finger as a brush, he wrote only a few characters. He rolled the snippet of cloth tightly until it resembled a piece of string and then knotted it securely around the bird's foot. With a squawk and a flap of wings, the crow flew off.

And so it came to pass that Tswei Ching was startled out of his afternoon nap in the courtyard of his house by the cries of the crow. The excited bird dipped and rose a number of times before it landed at his feet. Flapping its wings and prancing about in an agitated state, it succeeded in attracting Tswei Ching's attention to the string wrapped around its foot.

Ever so gently, Tswei Ching untied the piece of cloth, smoothed it out and read, "In prison!" It was unmistakedly Wen's handwriting. Tswei Ching knew his son was in grave danger and that he must go to him without delay. With a heavy heart, Tswei Ching set out for Kaifeng.

On the outskirts of the city, he was approached by a beggar. Before he could reach into his purse, the beggar cried out, "Master, Master!" Tswei Ching recognized the servant who had accompanied Wen to the capital. Sorrowfully the servant disclosed to his master the treachery of Liu Ying.

Tswei Ching decided to go directly to the *yamen*, where he would seek the counsel of the wise Lord Bau. Armed with his servant's witnessed account of what had happened, he was eager to present his complaint against Liu Ying.

"I deem the charges extremely serious," declared Lord Bau. "Devotion to one's family is a sacred duty. I shall seek to unmask your adopted son's outrageous conduct."

It was not an easy task that Lord Bau had set for himself. Liu Ying was a royal advisor, trusted by the emperor. To accuse him of unprincipled conduct and perchance set off a court scandal carried many risks. Lord Bau thought long and hard about a way to expose Liu Ying's knavery.

Lord Bau sent a messenger bearing a note to Liu Ying.

"I ask that you join me for dinner tomorrow evening." Flattered by the invitation from the noble judge, Liu Ying was happy to accept.

Liu Ying arrived at the judge's home attired in his best official gown. The delicious meal and the pleasant conversation with Lord Bau left him sated and cheerful. The more wine he drank, the more expansive his mood became.

At an opportune moment Lord Bau steered the conversation toward Liu Ying's personal life.

"I am interested to know about your family. Your parents must be proud indeed to have raised such an accomplished son."

Basking in Lord Bau's attention, Liu Ying warmed to his subject and regaled his host for over an hour with exaggerated tales of his adopted family. When he came to the part about the Queen Mother's seal, he repeated the same lie he had told the emperor. As for sharing the reward with his brother, he made no mention of it at all.

"You tell me," continued Lord Bau, "that Tswei Ching is wealthy. You must have lived in a great house with many servants."

"Oh, yes," eagerly agreed Liu Ying, thrusting out his chest with pride. "My father provided the best tutors for my brother and me. He treated me as though I were of his own flesh and blood, equal to his number one son, Wen."

"Where is your brother now?" asked Lord Bau in an offhand manner.

"My brother lives at home in splendid luxury. He is not burdened with responsibilities and leads a carefree life of pleasure." Liu Ying continued to build his tower of lies.

"Do you sometimes wish that you, who are so bowed down with government duties, could exchange your life for your brother's life of ease?"

"I would gladly welcome such an opportunity," said Liu Ying with a sigh.

Rarely given to displays of emotion, Lord Bau smiled wanly and replied, "You shall have your wish, for you have certainly earned it."

At a signal, Lord Bau's aide opened a door at the rear of the room. Tswei Ching and Wen entered. The brothers glared at each other. No word passed between them.

Lord Bau nodded his head in the direction of two guards. They stepped forward and stationed themselves at either side of the hapless Liu Ying.

"Remove his hat," barked Lord Bau.

"Remove his hat," barked Lord Bau.

Stripped of the symbol of his authority, his betrayal exposed, Liu Ying knew that he had fallen into Lord Bau's well-laid snare. As he was being led away, he heard Lord Bau say, "See that he is provided with the same living conditions and comforts that his brother enjoyed."

Snow White Goose

When the slanting beams of the sun's first light peeked through the window and touched his quilt, Changtsai, most trusted servant to his master, Geng Kun, stretched, yawned, and slowly rolled his plump body over to his other side. Drugged with sleep, he kept both eyes tightly shut, pretending daylight had not yet come and that he still had hours more to slumber.

"Time to rise, time to rise, Changtsai," the cook was nudging him. "Hurry, the master sent me to tell you he is awaiting your arrival. It is well past the first crow of the brown cockerel, and he is already breakfasting. Go to him at once!"

Changtsai groaned. Vaguely he recollected that last evening Geng Kun had ordered him to appear at his breakfast table for instructions concerning a particular errand. "What does he want from me now?" Changtsai thought crossly. "And so early in the morning! Lately, every day he finds some especially unpleasant chore for me. What a nuisance is the master!"

Although every bone in his body yearned for sleep, Changtsai, moaning as if he were in great distress, urged his corpulent body to a sitting position. Clumsily he rose to his feet, but once upright, he moved with more agility. Changtsai pulled his baggy trousers over his protruding belly, donned a clean loose jacket, slipped his feet into straw sandals, and headed for Geng Kun's quarters.

He found his master noisily slurping down a bowl of steaming hot rice gruel. Changtsai's stomach began to rumble. He was more annoyed than ever with this early appointment.

"Master," Changtsai veiled his irritation with a silver tongue, "I come before you, as you requested, to receive my orders and do as you bid."

"You have arrived on time, and that is a good thing, for the sooner you leave, the sooner you will return." A thin stream of gruel oozed from the corners of Geng Kun's mouth and ran down his chin.

Irked further by his master's slovenly eating habits, Changtsai found it most difficult to mask his displeasure. Yet he restrained himself, as all good servants must, and answered quietly, "I shall do whatever you wish, my master."

Geng Kun took his time. He finished eating, belched, smacked his lips with pleasure, and only then did he explain.

"Today is the birthday of my father-in-law, Li Chun, and I must send some gifts to his home near Kaifeng. I have chosen you to deliver them."

Changtsai paled. He hated walking long distances. His portly body rebelled at every step. From Tongan to Li Chun's home was a distance of more than twenty *li*, and then another twenty *li* back again. It would be almost high noon by the time he reached his destination, and dusk before he returned. A shiver of fear went through him. After sunset, the road crawled with bandits and murderers looking for likely victims such as he.

"Master, what gifts have you prepared for me to deliver to your father-in-law?" Changtsai kept his voice steady, his expression bland. Now Geng Kun had not been endowed with a generous nature, and Changtsai was well aware of his master's stinginess. Often he had heard him scolding the cook for discarding putrid fish. His gifts were never offerings given from the heart but only from a sense of obligation. So Changtsai chuckled inwardly when his penurious master informed him he was to deliver to Li Chun three gifts: one catty of noodles, some dried dragon-eye fruit, and a dozen steamed buns in the shape of peaches.

Changtsai had served his master faithfully for many years, and Geng Kun, knowing him to be the most intelligent and responsible of his many servants, took no offense when his underling offered a suggestion.

"Would it not be more appropriate to add one more gift? It is customary to send an even number. Besides, Master Li, being a proper gentleman, will no doubt return one or two of them, along with his gracious thanks. Remember, on your last birthday he generously gave you a bolt of the finest silk."

Before the day was over, Changtsai was to regret again and again that he had meddled in his master's business.

After a moment's pause, during which Geng Kun considered his servant's remark, he came to a decision. "When you go to the kitchen to pick up your bundles, tell the cook to catch my favorite white goose and put her into a bamboo basket. You will present the goose along with the other gifts to my father-in-law."

Changtsai's surprise at his master's fit of generosity gave way to a smirk when Geng Kun added, "But you must find a way to discourage the old man from accepting the bird. I have been fattening her for a banquet. See that you return with her unharmed."

Instantly Changtsai understood that he had made a grievous error. He should never have mentioned a fourth gift. And by what pretense could he succeed in preventing Li Chun from accepting the only decent present offered?

Changtsai was overcome with a premonition of disaster.

Vividly he pictured himself returning home in the dark of night, empty-handed, growing more fearful with each step lest thieves lying in wait kill him and toss his bloodied body into a clump of weeds.

Yet Changtsai never shirked his duty. He hurried to the kitchen and hastily consumed two warm millet buns with his cup of hot tea. Then he instructed the cook to place the noodles, fruit, and buns in lacquered boxes. He and the cook went together into the yard, easily captured the unsuspecting white goose, shoved her into a bamboo basket, and latched the lid. To one end of his

Changtsai shouldered his pole with its dangling baskets of gifts.

carrying pole Changtsai tied the lacquered boxes, and to the other the caged goose. Balancing the pole across his broad shoulders, he was ready for the tedious journey.

Once he started down the road, Changtsai grew less apprehensive. High above him, fleecy white clouds crept leisurely across a cerulean sky. He listened to a lone hawk whistling for his mate. In the fields he passed, reapers were cutting soy beans and gathering sheaves of golden wheat. Changtsai felt unfettered, free. Only when the white goose attempted to push her head through a small opening near the top of the basket did Changtsai's anxiety return. He was reminded of the absurd task that lay before him. It would be impossible to convince Li Chun not to accept this healthy, fine-feathered fowl.

By mid-morning Changtsai had covered a good distance. No longer did he have the road to himself. Carts heaped with vegetables rolled by, headed in the direction of the city marketplace. Weighted down by overflowing baskets hung from their carrying poles, farmers trotted past him in their rhythmic gait. Fleet-footed carriers dodged their way through the milling crowds bearing wealthy gentry in elaborate sedan chairs to their social appointments. Far from his master, enjoying the hubbub around him, Changtsai nodded pleasantly to other travelers. In return, some of them paused to admire his handsome goose. Why, it was turning out to be a fine day after all!

A delicious odor reached Changtsai's nose. It reminded him that he had eaten very little for breakfast. He yearned for some food to satisfy his hunger and a bowl of wine to slake his thirst. The peevish goose, resigned to her imprisonment, had become silent. She, too, needed a handful of grain and a little water. He felt sorry for her.

The aroma grew stronger when Changtsai neared an open stall where refreshments were being sold, but he had to pass it by. Not one coin did he have with him, and he was too proud to ask for charity like a beggar. To add to his discomfort, the breeze had ceased and tiny flying insects buzzed about his head. His legs felt heavy and his pace slowed to a crawl. He would have welcomed a shady spot where he could set down his pole and rest. He reminded himself that he had gone more than half way and would reach his destination by midday, and he further bolstered his spirits by imagining he would find a cool pond beyond the next curve.

When at last he did round a bend, he found not a pond but a calamity. A cart that had tipped over onto its side at the edge of the road lay surrounded by melons, some whole, some split, many squashed. The braying donkey, entangled in the reins, was desperately trying to free himself. The driver was missing. Forgetting his thirst, forgetting his weariness, Changtsai set down his burdens by the roadside. Quickly he freed the donkey and tied him to the nearest tree. Surely, he reasoned, the driver had been thrown clear of the cart. Perhaps he was injured, or worse still, was lying dead, nearby.

Frantically pushing apart the tall, thin stalks of ripe wheat, Changtsai cried out again and again, "Ho there. Is there someone about?" It was only after he stumbled over the farmer's inert body that he found him. Changtsai gently rolled him over on to his back and put his hand on the farmer's forehead. It felt warm, a good sign of life.

Changtsai patted him softly on both cheeks, repeating, "Wake up, wake up. I am here to help you." To Changtsai's great relief, the man's eyelids twitched, then opened. With a perplexed look on his face, the farmer regarded the stranger.

"Who are you? Where am I?"

"You were thrown from your cart into this field during an unfortunate accident. But, happily, it does not seem that you have been badly injured. I am here to offer assistance whenever you feel strong enough to rise."

Once up on his feet with Changtsai's help, the farmer became aware of the extent of the damage. On the verge of hysteria, he cried, "Where is my donkey? My melons are ruined! I am done for!"

"Your donkey is safe, and tied to a tree." Changtsai spoke softly, hoping to calm the frantic driver. "See him over there? He is perfectly fine. Come, we will right your cart together and reload it with the remaining undamaged melons. You can harness the donkey and be on your way to the market. The day is still young. There will be time to sell your produce and make a fine profit."

"I do not know how to thank you," the farmer said to Changtsai with sincere feeling. "Until I sell my melons, I have no money to pay you for your kindness, but please accept my largest melon."

In the excitement, Changtsai had forgotten how tired and thirsty he was, and if the white goose had not begun to hiss and honk without surcease, he would have forgotten her, too. The farmer presented him with a melon so ripe and sweet-smelling he could barely wait to taste it. With a friendly pat on the shoulder, Changtsai bade the farmer a good day, wishing him much luck and a safe journey.

Changtsai broke open the melon and lifted a piece to his mouth. He bit into it and let the delicious sweet juice trickle down his parched throat. Hungrily he sank his teeth into the firm flesh, throwing the rind and seeds to the goose. The thirsty bird, upon receiving such an unexpected treat, fluffed out her feathers and pecked away contentedly.

Refreshed, Changtsai again shouldered his pole and continued on his way. He had not gone very far before he did come upon a sparkling pond. A stand of willow trees lined the bank, their gracefully drooping branches overhanging the clear water. A perfect place to take a much-needed rest. Good fortune was with him again.

Although the sun was past its zenith and he should not have wasted another minute, Changtsai welcomed the opportunity to remove his sandals, sit on the grassy bank and let his tired feet dangle in the shallow limpid water. Time crept by unnoticed while he watched with fascination a mother fish gracefully waving her tail back and forth as she hovered over the eggs she had laid in her bowl-shaped nest. A cool breeze came up, reminding him that the afternoon was waning and that he had better hurry along.

About to slip his feet into his sandals, he noticed a large mud-hole near the edge of the pond. A mischievous thought occurred to him. He would smear the white goose with mud. Surely Li Chun would reject a filthy bird. What a splendid way to fool his master's old father-in-law, and, at the same time, return home with the coveted bird in hand. Whereupon Changtsai reached down into the dark puddle and scooped up a handful of wet mud. With caution he lifted the lid of the bamboo basket and removed the goose. Holding her firmly, he plastered her white feathers with the soft muck. Satisfied that she was most unsightly, he pushed her back into the basket. Changtsai arrived at Li Chun's house confident of success.

"Master," Changtsai began, "your son-in-law, Geng Kun, has asked me to deliver these gifts on the occasion of your birthday. He regrets that he could not come himself today but hopes you will accept these modest offerings as a token of his esteem."

Changtsai could tell that Li Chun was pleased. He was not particularly fond of his son-in-law and sometimes regretted that he had agreed to marry his lovely daughter to a man renowned for being a miser. Now he had sent four presents. Perhaps Geng Kun was not so tight-fisted after all.

Li Chun did not fail to notice the goose in the bamboo basket. However, his eyesight was poor and he paid little attention to her soiled feathers. He expressed his appreciation for the gifts, but not wanting to appear overly eager, he told Changtsai to go to the kitchen and ask his cook to select two of the four gifts. He was certain that the cook would choose the goose and serve the succulent bird that very evening for his birthday feast.

When Changtsai walked into the kitchen, the cook was in the midst of preparing a special soup for the celebration. After a brief exchange of polite chatter, Changtsai slid the pole from his shoulder and set the gifts on the floor. Delighted with the prospect of choosing two presents, the cook was immediately attracted to the white goose. "What have we here?" he asked, poking his nose close to the basket. "Well, if it isn't a goose, perfect for tonight's supper. But there is something wrong with her. I have never seen a goose with such strange dark spots on her feathers."

To the cook Changtsai replied, "She seemed perfectly well when I left Tongan early this morning."

"Let me have a look at her," suggested the cook. "In my trade I have handled many birds and can usually tell what ails them." Changtsai could think of no reason to refuse the cook's innocent request and placed the basket on the table.

The cook unlatched the lid. Reaching in, he grasped the goose firmly by the feet and pulled her out. He examined her closely. "Why are her feathers so dirty?"

The hapless bird, trying to free herself, flapped her wings. For a split second the cook carelessly loosened his grip. The goose twisted her neck, pecked savagely at his face, broke from his grasp, and started to fly wildly about the kitchen. Bits of caked mud dropped off her feathers, splattering the walls, the floor, and most unforgivable, plopping into the boiling pot of water which the cook had readied to make his master's soup. The enraged cook caught the bird by her feet in mid-air, slammed her savagely on the table, grabbed a cleaver, and in one powerful stroke chopped off her head. He threw the muddied carcass into the steaming cauldron and shouted victoriously, "My master will not have soup tonight but he will eat fresh goose!" The cook pulled the dripping bird out of the pot and set about plucking her feathers.

Changtsai was overcome with a feeling of revulsion. He stood transfixed, gaping at the goose's bloodied head lying on the table. One wide-open vacant eye stared directly back at him as if blaming him for her untimely death. Feathers were still floating in the air all around him. One tickled Changtsai's nostril and he gave a great sneeze. He could take no more. Snatching up the empty basket, he fled in panic.

He ran without stopping until he could scarcely catch his breath. Near an old tree stump, he decided to rest for a while. "What am I to do?" he moaned. "If I do not return home, there is nowhere I can go. And if I do return home, I will be soundly thrashed. Not only have I lost the goose, the carrying pole also remains behind." But there was no use putting off the inevitable. He had to face Geng Kun sooner or later. Changtsai picked himself up and, with leaden feet, continued his trek homeward.

Changtsai could not tell how long it took him to reach the small pond where he had earlier stopped to soak his feet. He had not intended to stop there again except that he caught sight of a flock of geese in an open field on the other side of the road. His heart leaped, for he hoped he would find a replacement for the goose he had lost. Intently he studied them. At first they all appeared to be brown or speckled. Disappointed, he was about to move along when he spied one standing somewhat apart from the others. She was plump and beautiful, and best of all, her feathers were milky white.

"Luck is with me today!" rejoiced Changtsai.

By now it was late in the afternoon and the road was almost deserted. As noiselessly as he could, Changtsai crept up behind the white goose, who was busily occupied gleaning the harvested field. It seemed as though she would be an easy catch. Holding his breath, Changtsai cautiously reached for her. The startled goose squawked with alarm and flew to the shallow end of the pond. She skittered along the glistening surface and hid in a clump of reedy grasses.

Without wasting even a second to remove his sandals, Changtsai hurried after her. His feet sank into the spongy bottom of the pond. Changtsai's heart nearly missed a beat for he thought he had lost her. But he had despaired too soon. Just as he was about to turn away, the goose poked her yellow beak out from among the stalks. With a mighty lunge forward, Changtsai grabbed her between his hands. Honking loudly and straining to spread her wings, the frightened bird fought to free herself of his clutches. Once she was subdued, he carried her to dry land and tried to shove her into the empty basket.

Regrettably, Asan, caretaker of his master's geese, was about to round up the strays that had wandered away from the flock. He missed the white goose and wondered what had become of her. A loud squawking caught his ear and then he saw a stout man hastily shoving the protesting bird into a bamboo basket.

"Stop, thief! That's my goose," Asan shouted. "What do you

think you are doing?" The incensed keeper rushed at Changtsai. He grasped the basket and tried to pull it away. Changtsai did not let go.

Pretending innocence, Changtsai answered, "Why are you so upset? This is my master's goose. I just let her out for a moment so she could quench her thirst. She is very tame."

"You are a liar as well as a thief. There is only one white goose in my flock and she has disappeared. You have stolen her. Hand her over!"

"I will not. She does not belong to you," Changtsai insisted.

The commotion soon attracted many onlookers who gathered about the two angry men.

"How can you be certain the goose is yours?" called one of the spectators to Asan.

"You're a thieving poacher," another accused Changtsai.

Sides were drawn as more stragglers joined in, some in favor of Asan, some in favor of Changtsai. The two contenders, one heavy and strong, the other quick and agile, continued their name-calling while tugging fiercely at the bamboo basket. A few more tugs and the basket would have been torn apart. Asan brought the fight to an abrupt end by kicking Changtsai in the groin. Changtsai doubled over in pain and the basket fell to the ground.

At that moment, fate intervened.

An ornate sedan chair hove into view. The carriers halted and lowered it. From behind the parted curtains, Lord Bau's face appeared. As soon as his aide, Ma Han, helped him to step down, the distinguished judge was recognized by everyone. The noisy throng fell silent.

Stiffly erect, with serious mien, Lord Bau demanded to know what was going on. Changtsai and Asan hung their heads sheepishly. In the presence of Lord Bau they did not dare resume their squabbling.

Asan was the first to attempt an explanation.

"The white goose belongs to my master's flock. I am Asan, his servant. I saw him," he said, pointing accusingly at Changtsai, "trying to steal her. Please tell him to give her back to me."

Lord Bau demanded to know what was going on.

"Most Honorable Judge, he is not telling the truth," Changtsai argued. "The goose belongs to my master. I, Changtsai, am taking her back to Tongan."

"It is not so, Honorable Judge," contended Asan. "When I came to collect my master's flock, the white goose was missing. I chanced to look across the road and I saw this rascally thief shoving the goose into a basket."

"That man lies," shouted a loud-mouthed spectator.

"No, no, he speaks the truth. I know the fellow well," contradicted another voice in the crowd.

Lord Bau raised his hand. "Silence!" he commanded. "I will get to the bottom of this without your uncalled-for advice."

Lord Bau did not take long in solving the dispute. He ordered those assembled to step back. His aide, Ma Han, was instructed to move the caged goose into the center of the cleared space. Changtsai and Asan were told to stand at either side of the basket.

"What do you feed your geese?" Lord Bau asked the keeper.

"My master owns many large fields, My Lord. The geese are permitted free range to eat the young green grass."

Turning to Changtsai, Lord Bau posed the same question.

"My master resides in the city. He keeps but a few geese for his table to be eaten on special feast days. They are penned up in a corner of the courtyard and stuffed with grain."

Lord Bau called for his aide, Ma Han, to step forward.

"Open the basket and sweep out all the old droppings at the bottom," he directed, "but do not let the bird escape. Then set the basket near my chair."

Within a short time the goose bespattered the floor of the basket with a copious quantity of fresh droppings. Lord Bau peered into the basket. The crowd edged closer. Heads craned to see what the judge was looking at.

"Move back, move back," snapped Ma Han.

"This goose is rightfully claimed by the keeper Asan." Lord Bau's declaration left everyone wondering how he had come to that decision.

"As for you," said Lord Bau, fixing his gaze on Changtsai,

"you are nothing but a common thief. Twenty-five strokes with a bamboo stick will help you remember never to steal again and never to conceal your evil deeds with lies."

Bravery was not one of Changtsai's strongest qualities. The thought of not being able to sit on his bruised buttocks brought him to his knees.

"Have mercy, My Lord, I know I have done wrong and deserve to be punished, but there were circumstances that made me stray from the path of honesty. I beg you to listen to my side of the story."

"You may speak, but remember," Lord Bau warned Changtsai, "no matter what you say, it will not erase your guilt, nor will you escape paying the penalty for your wrongdoing."

In relating the events that led him to steal the white goose, Changtsai's remorse and contrition were apparent.

"In truth, your master assigned you an impossible task." Changtsai's misery aroused Lord Bau's sympathy. "Instead of twenty-five blows, you will receive fifteen, enough to be a stern lesson for you, one that you will not easily forget."

And so Changtsai bared his bottom, and Lord Bau's aide delivered the beating. Changtsai's layers of fat protected him, and he was not severely hurt. Yet he had endured a painful humiliation and he wished to compose himself before moving on. Thus it was that he overheard Ma Han ask Lord Bau on what evidence he had so easily found in favor of Asan and against Changtsai.

"It is quite simple. If the goose belonged to Changtsai, she would have been raised in Tongan, in the courtyard of a city house. She would have been fed grain, and her manure would be yellow. Asan's goose ran freely in the fields and ate nothing but grass. Had you examined the manure in the bottom of the basket, you would have seen that it was green. What goes in green at one end comes out green at the other."

The aide let out a lusty guffaw. "Imagine, manure acting as a witness in solving a crime!"

More discouraged than ever, Changtsai trudged his way homeward.

"My life is not worth a pinch of sand," he grieved. "Darkness will descend before I reach home. Lurking cutthroats will do me in and I have not the strength to fight them off. If by a stroke of good fortune I succeed in returning unharmed to Tongan, my sore bottom will suffer again from a beating worse than the first." Changtsai was heart-sick with self-pity.

The bustling of the day had given place to the quiet of the evening. The road was deserted. From a distance, Changtsai heard the rumble of an approaching cart. The driver reined in his mule alongside the lonely walker.

"It is good to meet you again," he called out, recognizing Changtsai. "Perhaps this time I can be of help to you."

With sincere gratitude, Changtsai looked into the kindly face of the farmer.

"Climb up," said the farmer cheerfully. "There is plenty of space. The wagon is empty, for I have sold every one of my melons. I shall be happy to take you home."

On the way to Tongan the farmer insisted that Changtsai accept a piece of silver. "It is the very least I can do to repay you for saving my life."

Upon his return home, Changtsai went directly to his room. Wearily he stretched out upon his straw mat. In the stillness of the night, peace came to the troubled servant. A faint smile crept over his round face. He was dreaming that his stingy master could not thank him enough for exchanging a mere goose for a piece of silver.

Palace Plot

How was it that Jan Dzung, the powerful emperor of the Middle Kingdom who ruled over China with a mandate from heaven awakened every morning feeling downcast and melancholy? The birds sang in the garden outside his bedroom door, fresh dew glistened in the early rays of the sun, and flowers opened their petals, joyously welcoming the day. But the emperor paid little heed to the beauty around him. He was not content, for he had no heir to inherit his throne.

During the early years of his reign, Emperor Jen Dzung had devoted himself entirely to his far-flung empire and had won high praise for the way he dealt with affairs of state. From the beginning, he had the wisdom to surround himself with loyal ministers and men of great learning. Guided by their wise counsel, he undertook many ambitious projects that brought prosperity and peace to his subjects. He was so preoccupied with official business that he neglected to select a wife. Instead, as was customary, he had taken two concubines, Lady Li and Lady Liu.

Jen Dzung was captivated by Lady Li's dark, almond eyes, by her peach-blossom complexion and rose-bud lips. He admired her shining black hair, piled into an elaborate bun atop her head and held in place by a carved jade comb. Always considerate and gentle, Lady Li was able to soothe the emperor's troubled mind whenever he was in her company.

Lady Liu delighted the emperor with her lively conversation

and high spirits. Her sparkling eyes and bubbling laughter endeared her to him. When he was with her she entertained him by singing sweet songs, accompanying herself on the lute.

The day came when the emperor, older and concerned about the future welfare of his kingdom, summoned them both into his chambers. When they were seated comfortably and had been served a cup of tea, he explained that he wished to speak to them about a matter of great importance.

"My constant worry," he began, "is that I shall have no heir to take my place when I am gone. I think about it night and day, and it grieves me that I do not have a son to follow after me. I have always cherished the hope that my dynasty would continue unbroken for generations. Today," continued Jen Dzung, "an idea has come to me. I believe that my hope can be realized, but only with your cooperation."

Lady Li and Lady Liu glanced at each other. It was plain from the expression on their faces that his talk puzzled them.

Lady Li bowed respectfully. "I am honored, Your Excellency, that you ask for my assistance." Smiling shyly, she added, "I shall be glad to help in any way I can."

"And I, too," agreed Lady Liu, "am always ready to do whatever you ask."

Thus assured, Jen Dzung disclosed his plan to them. "The time has come when I should take a wife. I feel a deep affection for both of you, and I find it impossible to make a choice. Therefore, I have decided that whoever will be first to present me with a male child shall be given the title of Queen, and shall reign beside me on the royal throne."

Emperor Jen Dzung could not foresee that his words would stir up a bitter rivalry between his two concubines, one that would cause untold suffering and claim many victims, he himself among them.

Before long, Lady Li learned that she was pregnant. It was predicted by the court fortune-teller that the child would be a boy. The emperor was overjoyed, and in appreciation he presented Lady Li with a brooch of gold and precious jewels in the shape of a phoenix.

With the passing of each month, the air of expectation in the palace mounted. In anticipation of the eventful day, elaborate preparations were underway to receive the royal prince.

Lady Liu remained apart. Resentful of the attention centered on Lady Li, she spent most of her time sulking in her own quarters. Bitterness assailed her when she realized she would never sit upon the royal throne. If only there were a way to alter the course of events! She sought out Guo Huai, her favorite palace eunuch. Perhaps he could advise her.

Guo Huai had lived in the palace since he was a child. Sharp of mind, cunning and crafty, he went about ingratiating himself with the emperor by wearing a false smile and catering to Jen Dzung's every whim. Well aware that the emperor favored both Lady Li and Lady Liu, Guo Huai had encouraged their friendship. With Lady Li, who was modest and reserved, he did not succeed, but with the more outgoing Lady Liu, he developed a sympathetic relationship. They conversed frequently, and often found themselves exchanging confidences. So it was perfectly natural for Lady Liu to turn to Guo Huai to unburden herself.

When she poured out her heart, Guo Huai consoled her. "Your sadness pains me, but do not fret any longer. I promise I will think of something to restore your good humor. Even now, as you speak to me, thoughts are forming in my head. Meanwhile, keep a cheerful appearance and let no one suspect that you are troubled."

Guo Huai's confidence encouraged Lady Liu. She trusted him. Still, she worried that something might go awry, exposing both of them to the wrath of the emperor. For her the next few months were filled with anxiety.

The palace gong announced the good news. An heir to the throne had been born. The infant was quickly wrapped in layers of soft cloth and taken to the nursery. Lady Liu, worn out by the long, painful labor and feeling very weak, fell asleep immediately. Toward evening when she awoke somewhat refreshed, she asked the nursemaid in attendance to bring her the baby. The nursemaid placed a tightly wrapped bundle on the bed beside Lady Li, who expectantly undid the silken brocade wrapper.

Lady Li stared in disbelief. Instead of a healthy baby boy there lay a jelly-like mass of pink flesh. Green eyes stared unseeing from a shriveled head. Small pointed ears like those of a cat stuck out above the skull. Piercing screams rose from Lady Li's throat and echoed through the rooms of the palace. Her pitiful cries gave way to hysteria, and she lapsed into unconsciousness.

The emperor was informed that Lady Lie had given birth to a monster! His disappointment soon turned to anger, and he blamed the poor mother for having produced such an unnatural creature. Declaring that he never wanted to see her again, he banished her to the servants' quarters.

During all this turmoil, Lady Liu and Guo Huai closeted themselves in Lady Liu's sitting room. Several pillows had been arranged on a small bench, and on this makeshift crib an infant was fast asleep. Guo Huai was explaining, " . . . and then I killed the cat with one blow, skinned it, patted it dry and wrapped it up. Undetected by anyone, I stole into the nursery and exchanged one bundle for the other." Guo Huai smiled with self-satisfaction.

Lady Liu was shaken by the audacity of Guo Huai's scheme. She was now involved in a plot from which she could not extricate herself.

"What am I to do with the baby?" she cried.

"This is no time for whimpering!" The brash eunuch was plainly annoyed. His icy tone frightened Lady Liu.

"Have him killed and be done with it," he said without a trace of feeling.

Lady Liu felt trapped. Even if she wanted to undo everything that had happened, it was impossible. Finally, when she could think of no alternative, she called for her personal maid, Pearl, and ordered her to drown the baby in the river that ran close to the palace grounds.

Always dutiful, Pearl had never before disobeyed Lady Liu's bidding. Now, as she carried the baby toward the river, rebellion rose within her for the first time. She could not take a life. She could not make herself obey her mistress's instructions. Clutching the infant to her chest, she walked slowly. Her eyes were

Undetected by anyone, Guo Hai stole into the nursery
and exchanged the newborn babe for a cat.

swollen, her cheeks tear-stained. She felt more wretched with every step. At her wit's end, she sat down on the damp ground. So absorbed was she in her misery she did not hear the sound of approaching footsteps.

Chen Lin, one of the emperor's most trusted eunuchs, was at her side. He was on his way to deliver a bowl of fresh fruit to the emperor's cousin, Duke Jau. "Why are you crying?" Chen Lin asked.

Pearl felt that she need not fear betrayal at Chen Lin's hands. He was respected by everyone in the palace for his high moral character. Haltingly, she told him about the events that had led up to her present plight. The kindly eunuch was shocked by Pearl's story. He found it hard to believe that such vile acts were taking place under the emperor's roof. He helped Pearl to her feet.

"Enough weeping," he said firmly. "It won't do to have someone see you with such red eyes. We must act without delay." A faint cry came from the bundle. The infant was beginning to stir.

Chen Lin loosened the paper seal that secured the cover of the bowl. He quickly removed the cover and discarded the fruit. "Give me the baby," he directed.

"What are you going to do with him?" Pearl asked anxiously.

"I shall take him with me to Duke Jau's house. He and his wife are childless, and I am certain a baby boy will bring joy into their lives. Now, Pearl, you must run back to the palace and tell Lady Liu that you have carried out her orders. Go as fast as you can, and remember, only you and I know the truth."

Chen Lin placed the baby in the bowl and reset the cover lightly. He wiped the sweat from his forehead and hurried on, hoping to reach the Duke's house without incident.

He had not gone very far when directly into his path stepped the huge Guo Huai.

"Have you seen Pearl?" he asked Chen Lin gruffly.

"No, I have not seen her today," Chen Lin replied with dignity.

"What are you carrying in that bowl?" Guo Huai persisted.

"On behalf of the emperor, I am delivering this bowl of fresh fruit to Duke Jau. Today is the duke's birthday." Chen Lin forced himself to smile.

"Give me that bowl," came the haughty demand. "I want to see what is in it myself." Guo Huai tried to grab the bowl out of Chen Lin's firm grasp.

"Have you taken leave of your senses? This bowl was sealed by the emperor and no one but the duke may open it. If you dare touch this bowl once more, I shall report your inexcusable behavior to His Majesty." Chen Lin remained outwardly unperturbed while hiding his inner turmoil.

"Oh, little prince," implored Chen Lin silently, "please do not make a sound, or we shall all be dead." Unsettled by the close call, he walked quickly away without a backward glance.

Duke Jau and his wife welcomed Chen Lin warmly. After an exchange of greetings they asked what had brought him to their house.

Chen Lin held out the bowl and said, "I bring you a gift for your birthday." Duke Jau removed the cover of the bowl. His eyes widened when he saw the tiny infant curled up inside. Before the duke could ask for an explanation, Chen Lin recounted the tragic events that had occurred in the palace.

"I have brought the child here with the hope that in your home he will be sheltered and kept from harm."

The duke and his wife were enchanted with the pink-cheeked infant. By the time he reached his first year, the child was toddling easily on sturdy legs. At three he could be seen running through the garden chasing crickets and butterflies. From his mother, Lady Li, he had inherited an even temper, and like her, his sweet expression and friendly smile won him the affection of all. His mind flowered early, and when he was six, a fine tutor was hired to begin his training in the classics.

That same year the palace gong rang out a second time to announce good tidings. Lady Liu had given birth to a male child. The emperor rejoiced. He sent off messengers to carry the news to the most distant villages in the land. With all the pomp and splendor befitting such an occasion, Lady Liu was crowned queen.

Unfortunately, the baby sickened and died before he was three months old. A pall settled over the palace. Dispirited by the tragedy, the emperor shut himself in his study and refused to see anyone.

"Now I may never have an heir," he lamented.

Weeks passed and still the emperor continued to mourn. In search of solace, he decided to pay a call on his cousin, Duke Jau. In their youth both men had spent much time together, but due to the press of official business, years had slipped by without their seeing one another.

When the emperor arrived at Duke Jau's home he was cordially received. "It is indeed a great honor that you have come to pay us a visit," said the duke, "and I am grateful that you accept our hospitality."

The duke invited the emperor into the courtyard. The plum trees were at their showiest, each one a large bouquet of white blossoms. The sweet scent of pink peonies perfumed the air. In the midst of this serene landscape the emperor felt less dejected. He and the duke sat in the open pavilion, talking quietly of old times and sipping cups of hot tea.

Their conversation was interrupted by the appearance of a young boy who, the emperor assumed, was the duke's son. Accompanied by his tutor, the boy was about to take his daily walk in the fresh air. The emperor was completely taken by the handsome child.

Turning to Duke Jau, the emperor said ruefully, "For years I have cherished the hope of having an heir, and that wish is yet unfulfilled. I would gladly part with half my kingdom if only I could be blessed with a son like yours." The emperor hesitated. He chose his words carefully. "Would you be willing to allow the boy to come and live with me in the palace as my adopted son? I shall issue an official proclamation declaring that he will inherit the throne when I die. For the remaining years of my life I shall be content knowing that the dynasty will continue unbroken."

The emperor's request placed Duke Jau in an awkward predicament. He would have liked to reveal the truth about the boy. To disclose the palace plot, however, would implicate Queen Liu, and he doubted that his word would hold against her denial. To complicate matters further, he and his wife had grown extremely fond of the emperor's son. "We will miss him," Duke Jao thought sadly. But a royal request was a royal command. He had no choice.

"Your Majesty," he offered, nodding respectfully, "my wife and I are honored to grant your wish."

The boy was given over to the care of Queen Liu. At first she shared the emperor's joy. He had found a successor to the throne, and she had been given another chance to raise a son. But her happiness was short-lived, for almost immediately she noticed the strong resemblance the child bore to Lady Li. Buried memories came back to trouble her. She could not sleep, for her dreams were nightmares.

Once more Queen Liu sent for her loyal friend, Guo Huai, and told him of her growing qualms.

"What do you think I should do?" she questioned him tearfully. "How can we learn the truth?"

Guo Huai found the turn of events alarming. He recalled how Chen Lin had refused to open the bowl when they met along the river path. Could it be that the wily eunuch had deceived him and that Queen Liu's suspicions were justified? Dire thoughts raced through his head.

"Send for Pearl at once," he proposed, "and also for Chen Lin."

Within minutes, Pearl entered the chamber, followed by Chen Lin. Queen Liu wasted no time.

"Did you carry out my orders to drown Lady Li's baby?" she demanded of Pearl.

"Yes, Your Majesty," Pearl lied.

"Did you tell anyone about it?"

"Not a soul," she lied again, but her voice was beginning to tremble.

"Were you careful not to be seen?"

Pearl began to stammer a reply, but when she saw Guo Huai's piercing eyes fixed on her, she fell silent.

"Well," said Guo Huai, "if she will not talk, there is a way to loosen her tongue. A good beating often brings on a confession.

The happy emperor returns to the palace with his "adopted son."

May I suggest, Your Majesty, that you direct Chen Lin to apply a few strokes with bamboo rods. The pain in her back will hasten words from her mouth."

Queen Liu was desperate enough to fall in with this brutal idea, and Chen Lin had no choice but to comply. Not wanting to cause Pearl much pain, he picked up the rods and struck her lightly several times across the back. Guo Huai's steely eyes narrowed. "Harder," he shouted.

Chen Lin obeyed most unwillingly, and Pearl's wailing filled the chamber.

"That is not hard enough," raged Guo Huai. In a fit of fury he grabbed the rods out of Chen Lin's hand. Mercilessly, he rained blow after blow upon the hapless Pearl. "Now speak," he threatened. "You will not be spared unless you tell the truth. Did you drown the baby?" Pearl's lips remained sealed. Guo Huai bore down even harder, whipping the screaming Pearl until she crumpled at his feet.

"Enough, enough," cried Queen Liu. She was appalled by Guo Huai's ruthlessness and demanded he put down the rods. But it was too late. Pearl slowly raised her head. She looked directly at her tormentors and, in a barely audible voice, uttered her last words.

"You evil-minded devils, some day you will be punished for your wicked ways." A groan escaped her lips as she fell back on the floor. She had ceased to breathe.

Chen Lin understood that Queen Liu and Guo Huai would not be satisfied with just one victim. Fearing they would plan next to do away with Lady Li, he rushed to the servants' quarters to look for her. He found her at work in the kitchen, took her aside, and related all that had happened after the birth of her child.

"You must flee the palace," he warned, "for your life is in danger." He escorted her to safety beyond the palace gate and wished her good luck.

Outside the palace walls, Lady Li, once the beloved confidant of the emperor, was reduced to begging. With nothing but the clothes on her back, deprived of the flimsiest shelter, she determined to survive against all odds. "The time will come," she comforted herself, "when justice will prevail."

Emperor Jen Dzung reigned for ten more years before his allotted time on earth came to an end. He never learned that the boy whom he had adopted was his own son. With traditional pageantry, he was buried in an ornate tomb. In an equally splendid ceremony, the young emperor was seated on the throne and became the new ruler of China.

At that time the shrewd and righteous Lord Bau was serving as a judge in the capital. One day, when he was being carried across a small bridge leading to the palace gates, a disheveled dirty woman ran out in front of his sedan chair.

"Injustice, injustice!" she screamed. "The Queen Mother is an imposter. I am the emperor's mother, and I have evidence to prove it."

Lord Bau's curiosity was aroused and he motioned for his sedan chair to be set down. He spoke to his guard.

"Let the ragged beggar come closer so I can hear what it is that she wants."

"Your Excellency, I beg your indulgence," the woman pleaded. Her tone was now much quieter and she spoke with proper humility. "A great injustice was done to me many years ago. I am the true mother of the young emperor. Here, Your Excellency, is my proof." She handed the judge a small gold brooch in the shape of a phoenix.

Lord Bau inspected the unusual piece of jewelry, shaking his head in wonder. Such a gift could only be bestowed by the emperor, yet here it was, in the hands of this dirty beggar.

"Bring the woman to the *yamen*," he directed, and he gave the signal to move on.

That afternoon he was busy at his writing table when Lady Li was brought in. Politely, the judge asked her to be seated.

"You may leave us alone," he said, dismissing the guard.

Lord Bau listened with fascination to Lady Li's woeful tale. She told him how she had been mistreated and how she had been deprived of her child. Several times in the course of her narration she had to stop to fight back her tears.

This was a matter of extreme gravity. Since members of the royal family were involved, Lord Bau would have to handle the situation with the utmost delicacy. All the facts had to be established before informing the emperor.

The inquiry was begun by questioning Guo Huai. Naturally, the sly eunuch denied everything.

"You are willing to believe this deranged tramp instead of me," he protested. "You will never be able to prove so outrageous a charge."

"Very well," Lord Bau replied. "The woman may be deranged as you say, but until she is proven wrong I must hold you under arrest."

The judge's reputation for wisdom was well deserved, for he soon thought of an extraordinary plan. He had his courtroom rearranged to resemble a courtroom in hell. Incense was burned for hours, and a dense smoke hung heavily in the air. The court attendants were dressed in animal skins, grotesque masks of horned cow heads and full-maned horse heads hiding their faces.

When all the preparations were complete, the judge asked the warden to send a bottle of good wine and a bowl of delicious food to Guo Huai's cell.

"Tell the eunuch that the queen sends him a gift," the judge instructed the guard. Guo Huai was heartened by this lenient treatment. He took it as a sign that the queen would use her influence on his behalf and have him freed. With his stomach full of food and wine, he fell asleep, snoring loud enough to be heard throughout the jail.

At the stroke of midnight, his slumber was rudely shattered by the beating of bass drums. He sat up with a start. The drumbeats became faster and louder until he felt that his head was about to explode.

Then, above the din rose a blood-curdling shriek. Fully alert and very frightened, Guo Huai heard his name being called. Near him towered two masked attendants, their heads looking even more hideous as their horns cast elongated shadows on the walls. Guo Huai believed he was surely going mad.

The drums stopped suddenly. Out of the darkness came a low menacing voice.

"The day of justice has arrived. You will pay for all your past sins. You are condemned to suffer the tortures of hell and there will be no escape."

The roll of the drums sounded again. Guo Huai was jerked to his feet, and iron chains were wound around his neck. The attendants dragged him out of his cell, down the middle aisle of the long courtroom, and stood him before the judge. Now the eunuch was convinced he had awakened in Satan's domain.

"Bring Pearl into the courtroom," bellowed Lord Bau. Clad in the white robes of death, long black hair covering her face, a woman was led in. With slow deliberate steps she walked toward Guo Huai. The terrified eunuch recoiled as she came closer, and he would have fled had not the guards barred his way. In a high-pitched strident voice she accused him of unspeakable crimes.

"I am Pearl, the innocent maid you mercilessly beat to death. I have come to take my revenge. Your evil deeds have been disclosed, your villainy unmasked. Before the Judge of Hell, I charge you, Guo Huai, of plotting to kill the emperor's son."

"Please, Your Excellency," cried Guo Huai, falling to his knees. "It was not my fault. I was only following Queen Liu's orders." Words gushed from his mouth. When everything he had to say was properly recorded and his signature duly affixed, the judge ordered torches to be lit. The courtroom was flooded with light. Only then did Guo Huai realize that he had been tricked into a confession.

For his treachery Guo Huai was sentenced to death. He was executed on the night of the next full moon.

The wise Lord Bau continued to serve in the circle of the emperor's most loyal advisors. Those who were tempted to indulge in misdeeds desisted, knowing full well they would be found out and made to pay for their crimes. Thus justice prevailed throughout the land.

Tormented by remorse, Queen Liu fell ill. Secluded in her bedchamber, she would take neither food nor drink. She languished, and before the month ended, death claimed her.

The young emperor bestowed upon Lady Li the title of Queen Mother. Their reunion brought both of them great joy, and the emperor spared nothing to make his mother's life so pleasurable that in time she forgot her past suffering. With prudence and compassion he ruled for many years, earning the respect and devotion of his subjects.

> A palace plot has come undone,
> A mighty judge the truth has won,
> An inglorious end the wicked met,
> A dynasty, its course is set.
> The rightful king all subjects hail,
> Evil deeds will not prevail.

The Black Bowl

Nature had bestowed upon Sun Chyan a pockmarked face and a pair of oversized ears that stuck out grotesquely from either side of his head. Short of stature and stocky of build, with one shoulder higher than the other and one leg shorter than its partner, he hobbled along with a limp. Still single by the age of thirty-five, he had given up the possibility of marrying. For many years he lived alone in the city of Ding Jou earning his living as a potter.

Though a fine craftsman, working by himself Chyan turned out less than two dozen bowls each week. On market days, even if he sold out his entire stock, his income was barely enough to provide for his daily necessities. Hoping to increase his output, he decided to take as an apprentice a distant kinsman by the name of Sun Wan. The many long hours Chyan spent trying to teach Wan the art of molding a pleasing pot yielded little success. Neither bright nor capable, Wan was, nevertheless, an amiable companion who, in exchange for food and shelter, mixed the clay, kept the kiln fire stoked and swept the floor.

Freed of the time-consuming menial tasks, Chyan could produce more pieces of pottery to sell. His income increased, though not enough to offset the cost of feeding an extra mouth. Still, he never entertained the idea of sending Wan away, for he did not relish reverting to a life of solitude.

On an occasional evening, Chyan would permit Wan to accompany him to the ale house. There, he and his apprentice liked to imbibe a few cups of wine and exchange local gossip with acquaintances.

On such a night, after they had already finished two cups of delicious brew, a well-dressed stranger entered the ale house. His cloak, covered with fine dust, was fashioned out of sturdy cotton. His waist was girdled by an intricately woven belt, and upon his head he wore a hat made of expensive cloth. The stranger seated himself at a table, ordered food and drink, then paid for his refreshments with a silver piece. Chyan and Wan concluded he must be a man of considerable wealth. They struck up a conversation inquiring about his village, his travels, the nature of his work. As the evening wore on, the three men called for more and more wine. Well past the midnight hour they were still noisily exchanging tall stories. The innkeeper, wishing to retire, finally asked them to leave.

By now, the stranger was quite drunk. The wine had gone to his head, making it feel twice its normal size. When Chyan and Wan rose to leave, the stranger also made an effort to stand. So shaky were his legs, he dropped back into his chair. Unable to sit erect, his head fell forward, striking the edge of the table. He passed out and would have slipped off his seat had he not been restrained by his drinking partners.

"Let's take him outside," suggested Chyan. "Perhaps the cool night air will help him come to." Supporting the stranger under his arms, Chyan and Wan dragged him into the street. They held him upright and walked with him, hoping his feet would fall into step with theirs. Their drunken companion only grew heavier and heavier. When they reached the end of the street, they ducked into a dark alley and tried to prop his limp body against the wall of a building. He toppled over and lay senseless on the ground.

"Why not leave him here to sleep it off?" suggested Wan. "After all, he is no responsibility of ours." Wan started to walk away when Chyan called after him.

"Wait, if we abandon him in his present state, someone prowling about will be sure to come upon him and steal whatever money he has. Why let that happen when we could enjoy some extra cash ourselves?" Wan found the idea shocking.

"I have never stolen as much as a stalk of straw," he protested, "nor will I do it now."

"Be sensible," cajoled Sun Chyan, annoyed by Wan's squeamishness. "All I'm asking is that you help me a little."

They flipped the unconscious man over on his back. Careful not to make a sound, Chyan went through his pockets. They were disappointingly empty. His luck improved when he found a money belt tied securely around the stranger's waist. He slid from the belt a silk purse. It was heavy and there was no doubt that it contained a small fortune in gold or silver pieces.

"What a stroke of good luck we've had," Chyan murmured. "Yesterday we were poor, today we are rich!"

"Master," warned Wan, "when he wakes up and finds his money gone, he will suspect that we stole it. Surely, he will swear out a complaint against us before the prefect, and that will mean the end of the road for us."

"Then there is only one thing to do," retorted Chyan. "We have to kill him. A dead man keeps his silence forever."

Wan recoiled at the thought.

"You are such a simple-minded coward," Chyan sneered. "Once the man is dead, we can shove the body into the kiln. In a few hours there will be no trace of him. After that, we split the money, half for you, half for me." Reassured by his master's explanation, Wan agreed to participate in the plan without further complaint.

Chyan, in the lead, grasped the stranger's ankles, and Wan, in the rear, holding the stranger under the arms with both hands, started off for home at a slow jog. In the courtyard of their house, they set down their load. Chyan reached for an iron poker. With a single blow to the head, he sent the stranger's soul flying toward heaven.

"Don't stand there with your eyes popping," Chyan commanded. "Start a fire under the kiln." Wan obeyed meekly.

It proved to be an awkward task to fit the body into the heated interior. Pushing and squeezing, they finally managed to shove it in head first and latch the door. Throughout the long night they took turns adding fuel to the fire to keep it blazing hot. By the next morning all that was left of the stranger was a small pile of ashes.

"Do not discard the ashes," ordered Chyan. "I can make use of them." Chyan dumped the ashes into a batch of wet clay and kneaded the mixture until he was satisfied it was of a proper consistency. Taking more than usual care, he fashioned a large bowl. The bowl dried for several days before Chyan put it into the kiln for the first firing. After it cooled, he applied his best glaze, returning it to the kiln for a second firing. The finished bowl was perfect, without a flaw, deep and wide and shiny black.

"This will bring a good price," he boasted. Wan felt a great sense of relief. No trace of the evil deed remained.

Just as Chyan had predicted, the black bowl fetched a fine sum on the next market day. It was bought by old Uncle Wang, who admired its glossy finish and expected it would serve many useful purposes. And, indeed, it did. Old Wang used it to gather vegetables from his garden and to carry feed to his laying hens and his red rooster. When it rained, it served as a receptacle for collecting fresh water. The bowl proved to be a most versatile utensil.

One cold wintry night, old Wang was wakened out of his sleep by the urge to empty his bladder. Crawling out from under the warm covers on the *kang*, he staggered toward the door. Lately, he was finding it more and more uncomfortable to relieve himself in the frosty night air. He stepped outside. A blast of icy wind assailed his frail body from head to toe. Dressed only in his night clothes, he stood there, miserable and shivering, while the urgency to urinate grew almost unbearable. At that moment of extreme discomfort, Old Wang decided to use the black bowl for still another purpose. Moving back into the house, he slammed the door shut. He reached for the bowl on a shelf. But just as he began to enjoy relief, he was startled by a voice crying out in anger.

"How dare you squirt your yellow stinking filth into my mouth!" Old Wang drew back in alarm.

"Who is addressing me so rudely?" he wondered. "Did someone enter my house while I slept?" He groped around in the dark

The bowl was bought by Old Uncle Wang
who admired its glossy finish.

for his oil lamp and lit it. He shone the flickering light around the room, not missing a single corner. He opened cupboards, over-turned woven baskets, bent down to look under the table, stood on tiptoe, holding the lamp above his head to see if someone were hiding among the rafters. All in vain. No one was there. Old Wang returned to stand over the bowl and finish what he had started to do before he was interrupted.

"A plague upon your head! Why do you persist in your dis-gusting behavior?" It was the same voice he had heard before, only more agitated. Though he knew not to whom he was speaking, Old Wang asked, "Who are you and what do you want of me?"

"Hear me out. I am named Li Hau. I dwelt in Yang Jou. Last month on my way home from a business trip, I stopped to have some wine at an ale house near your city gates. Two shameful louts, potters by trade who go by the names of Sun Chyan and Sun Wan, plied me with drink until I was unable to stand on my own two feet. In the condition I was in, I could not fend them off. They robbed me. To hide their dastardly deed, they killed me, reduced me to ashes and mixed my remains with the clay from which your bowl was made."

Old Wang was dumbfounded. Was it possible that the bowl was talking to him? He dismissed the idea as ridiculous, but whoever it was had more to say.

"I am held fast in this bowl, unable to escape. Please, I be-seech you, bring my plight to the attention of Lord Bau. He will know how to bring the scoundrels to account."

Poor Old Wang! He was afraid he was losing his mind. He shook so from fright he was barely able to crawl back onto his *kang*. His mind raced around in circles, trying to sort out what had happened. The bowl had spoken. Of this he was certain. If a murder had truly been committed, the villains should not go un-punished. The honorable thing to do, he concluded, was to lay the whole matter before Lord Bau. He was the only one who would be able to get to the bottom of the mystery.

The very next day, carrying the bowl, Old Wang entered the *yamen*. He was granted an audience with the judge. Lord Bau listened to his story with amusement. Out of respect for Old Wang's gray hair, Lord Bau did not have him immediately thrown out.

A talking bowl! Lord Bau had dealt with foolishness and superstitions in his long career, but this was absurd. He doubted the elderly petitioner was sound of mind.

"Please, let the bowl speak for itself," humbly requested Old Wang.

"Very well," agreed Lord Bau. He would humor the doddering oldster.

"Tell the Honorable Judge your sad tale," encouraged Old Wang, tapping the bowl gently.

Silence.

"This is your chance to petition for justice."

Silence.

"Do not take up any more of my time with mindless babble," Lord Bau scolded, dismissing Old Wang with a wave of his hand.

Wang returned home confounded and unnerved. He set the bowl on a wide shelf above the *kang* and started to prepare his evening meal. A peculiar rattling sound made him turn around. The bowl was inching its way to the edge of the shelf. Old Wang lunged forward just in time to catch it.

"Sorry to disturb you," the bowl apologized. "I want to tell you how much I regret the trouble I have caused."

Old Wang was furious. "Now you can wag your tongue! Why didn't you speak up when Lord Bau questioned you?"

"Do not be angry. I ask your pardon for not being more cooperative. Try to understand. You carried me before the honorable judge unclothed. Being a modest man, I felt naked, terribly ashamed, and I could not bring myself to address him."

Old Wang scratched his head. He was truly exasperated, yet he and the bowl were developing an odd comradeship.

"Tomorrow," continued the bowl, "take me back to the *yamen*. Before we leave, be sure to wrap me in a cloth square. Then leave the rest to me."

"If it will please you," Old Wang agreed, as though speaking to a friend. "But you must promise not to play tricks on me."

Lord Bau listened to Old Wang's story with amusement.

Fortunately for Old Wang, the guards at the *yamen* gate were not the same ones who were stationed there on the previous day, else they would certainly have barred his way. Old Wang and his bowl had no difficulty entering a second time.

Engrossed in reading some important official papers, Lord Bau did not immediately take notice of the person who waited to be recognized. When he looked up and saw Old Wang, it was with considerable irritation that he asked, "Have you come again to tell me of your talking bowl?"

Wishing to let the bowl have its say, Old Wang made no reply. He set it on the floor, smoothing out the creases in the piece of cloth. Lord Bau did not know what to make of this perplexing character and his outlandish behavior.

"What does this mean?" he demanded, glaring at the mute Old Wang.

"Honorable Master, I do not wish to give offense. Neither does Old Uncle Wang. It is upon my insistence that he has brought me before you."

This time it was Lord Bau who remained mute, too stunned to react, for the voice was coming directly from the bowl.

"I understand your disbelief, and I hasten to offer an explanation. My name is Li Hau from the city of Yang Jou. I am dead, a victim of murder at the hands of Sun Chyan, the potter, and his apprentice, Sun Wan, who reside in your prefecture."

For the next few minutes, Lord Bau listened intently to the bowl's narration.

This was certainly the most extraordinary case Lord Bau had ever been called upon to resolve. His first impulse was to dismiss the unnatural tale as nonsense. Moreover, he did not wish to encourage the self-delusion of an aging codger such as Old Wang. Still, he refrained from making a hasty decision, for he could not positively rule out the murder charge. If the spirit of the traveler were indeed trapped within Old Wang's bowl, Lord Bau felt duty-bound to help set it free.

Chyan and Wan were sought out and brought in for questioning. Confronted with Old Wang's accusations, they denied everything. As could be expected, both swore they had never met the murder victim nor had they stolen his money. Chyan, pretending to be outraged, protested that his good name was being stained by untrue malicious charges. And Wan, aping his master, asserted with hurt dignity that he was a poor man, but honest and virtuous.

In spite of their claims of innocence, Lord Bau directed that they be detained. The narrow cell into which they were placed was damp and bone-chilling. It was bare of furnishings with the exception of a moldy bucket in one corner that smelled of human waste.

Chyan scanned the dimly lit cell with disgust. He resigned himself to being temporarily imprisoned. Distasteful though it was, he confidently believed he would soon be set free. Without a shred of evidence, even the astute Lord Bau would find it impossible to pin any guilt on him. Wan, by contrast, envisioned only the worst.

"It's all over for us," he whimpered. "We've been found out."

"Be quiet, you weak-kneed idiot!" snapped Chyan. "They can't prove a thing. No matter what accusations they hurl against us, I'll deny everything and you had better do the same." Wan winced.

"Do not fret so." Chyan bridled at his helper's meekness. "I have covered all our tracks. If we are accused of murder, there is no victim. If we are charged with theft, they can produce no proof. Who will ever be able to discover where the money is hidden?"

"I hope you are right," said Wan cheerlessly, not really convinced.

"Remember, keep a cool head," Chyan admonished, "and under no circumstances let on that the stranger's purse is hidden in an old cooking pot behind the *kang*."

Chyan's arguments did seem reasonable. Wan took heart. Perhaps all would turn out well.

"Depend on me not to weaken," he promised.

That night, Chyan and Wan found the earthen floor of their cell too hard and cold for comfort. They slept fitfully and were awakened early by the guard, who brought them each a bowl of thin millet gruel for breakfast.

A little while later, the guard came to collect the empty dishes. Curtly and without stating a reason, he ordered Wan to come along with him. Chyan started to follow after, but the guard pushed him back.

"Lord Bau has sent me to fetch only your helper."

For the first time, Chyan's self-assurance faltered. He had Wan's word that he would keep their secret, but he did not trust him completely. The cowardly simpleton might break down under Lord Bau's questioning. He paced the cell, growing frantic as the day wore on.

The clanging of the chain securing the cell door made Chyan jump, so tightly drawn were his nerves.

"Come with me. The judge will see you now."

It was already late afternoon. Chyan was marched to the front of Lord Bau's courtroom. A moment later, Wan was brought in through another door. Lord Bau looked down at the kneeling prisoners across a long table. In the center of the table stood Old Wang's black bowl. Next to it lay the murdered man's embroidered purse, emptied of its contents.

Chyan turned ghostly white. How he despised the cowardly Wan! That son of a toad must have betrayed him. The worthless clod has revealed everything!

In a fury, Chyan sprang at Wan, damning him with the vilest curses, while pummeling him with all his might. Not until Wan was beaten into unconsciousness did the guards intervene. They revived him with a splash of cold water.

Lord Bau addressed the accused.

"Sun Wan, you were an unwilling accomplice. Nevertheless, you should have known better than to blindly obey your master when he urged you to participate in his deviltry. You will receive fifty strokes with a heavy rod. Long will you remember the lesson it will impart.

"Sun Chyan, since you have made a full confession of robbery and murder, I am signing an order for your execution.

"Honorable Master, I do not recall having confessed to any crime."

"Indeed, you did divulge that you had killed a man and where you had hidden his stolen purse. My aide was stationed outside your cell at all times. Every word you spoke last night was overheard. Sun Wan remained loyal to you. It was you who gave yourself away. You have saved me and my staff much time and unpleasantness. We were able to locate the purse without difficulty."

Lord Bau proceeded to read the sentence.

"Rise! Sun Chyan of the city of Ding Jou, you are hereby condemned to death for taking the life of Li Hau, formerly of the city of Yang Jou. You do not deserve the least consideration, but I shall give you a chance to do one final good deed before you breathe your last. Perhaps the ruler of the next world will consider it when you are called to account for your earthly sins." Lord Bau motioned to a court attendant. The attendant lifted the bowl from the table and held it out before Chyan.

"Break it," commanded Lord Bau.

Chyan's jaw dropped. His hands shook uncontrollably. Terror clouded his eyes. He moved his hands forward to take hold of the bowl but quickly drew them back. Lord Bau lost patience.

"Break it, I say!"

The attendant shoved the bowl at Chyan, who had no choice but to grasp it. His trembling fingers could not hold on to it. Just as the bowl hit the ground, shattering into a multitude of pieces, Chyan felt a strong puff of wind blow past his face. Carried on the receding wind was a terse message from Li Hau.

"My cruel shackles are broken. At last, I am free to embark on my homeward journey. There, among my kinsmen, will my spirit dwell, at peace forever."

Borrowed Clothes

Jau Heng raised his cup of wine. "I drink to the happy union of our illustrious families."

"And I," countered Shen Lingmou, "am grateful that you deem my daughter worthy of your acceptance. With the help of heaven, may she bring happiness to your household by bearing many sons."

The two men, both prosperous merchants and old acquaintances, had just agreed to the betrothal of their young children. It would be ten years before the prospective bride and groom reached marriageable age, and though they would not meet before their wedding ceremony, they were considered man and wife until death.

The time of youth is fleeting. The day came when Shen, in a pensive mood, marveled how swiftly the years had flown. His frolicsome daughter, Ahwa, had passed her sixteenth birthday. She was a radiant beauty, considered by all to be the prettiest girl in the entire village.

Now Shen had to think seriously about preparations for her marriage. He planned to make Ahwa's wedding feast a most elaborate festive celebration. The guest list would number in the hundreds. Extra servants would be needed to prepare the many delicious foods. In anticipation of the occasion, he had long ago set aside ten jugs of the very best wine to insure the jollity of the merrymakers. All would be in readiness as soon as an auspicious date was determined.

At the home of Jau Heng, the happy day was also eagerly awaited. Arrangements to welcome a new daughter-in-law were almost complete. For the bride's family, gifts had been carefully selected, and for Ahwa, an exquisite bracelet of translucent jade had been chosen. It would be a personal present to the bride from her mother-in-law.

Jau Heng was very proud of his son, Yougwo. He had dutifully seen to the boy's education. Once his studies were completed, he would journey to the capital to take the civil service examinations. There was no doubt that he would pass the difficult tests with high grades and receive an appointment to a government post. Content that his son's prosperity was assured, Jau felt the girl Yougwo was about to marry was fortunate to have such a fine husband.

That year the spring rains began early. For days on end, dark clouds blocked out the sun and spilled out a steady downpour. In the western mountains, the melting snows sent streams of water cascading down the slopes. Gently flowing rivulets became roaring torrents. The muddy, silt-laden Yellow River rose steadily until it spilled over its banks. It was a signal to flee to higher ground.

Jau Heng's village lay nestled in a narrow valley beside a peaceful stream. Swollen by days of steady rain, the gently flow-ing stream escaped its banks, engulfing fields and homes. As though built of sticks, the sturdiest buildings toppled from their foundations into the rampaging waters. Jau's family lost all their worldly possessions. For years to come they would know the despair of poverty.

Shen was more fortunate than his friend. The flood waters did not reach his village which was perched high on a hillside. His family suffered no loss at all.

In spite of their long acquainceship, Shen showed little pity for his friend Jau. Now that Jau was poor, Shen no longer felt obliged to honor the betrothal agreement made long ago when circumstances were different.

"The wedding will not take place," he announced one evening at the dinner table. "What can Jau offer us? He is a ruined man. He will come empty-handed, bearing not a single gift for our family. I don't intend to give him a daughter-in-law without getting something in return." His words, issued in the manner of a final decree, shocked his family.

"This cannot be," his wife argued. "We shall all lose face and be shunned by everyone."

Shen, unaccustomed to having his authority as head of the family questioned, replied curtly and without feeling, "Jau is a ruined man. Besides, I have no intention of associating with someone beneath my station."

From a large platter, Shen picked up a piece of tender chicken with his chopsticks and brought it to his mouth. He continued to eat in silence, unruffled even when Ahwa, sobbing, fled to her room.

The following day, Shen had to leave for Loyang where he had some business to transact.

"I may be away for several weeks " he informed his wife. "When I return, I shall send word to Jau that the wedding has been called off."

Ahwa was especially distraught by her father's pronouncement. She believed his decision was scandalous. Yet, to challenge him was unthinkable. She brooded alone, imagining the scorn that would be heaped upon her parents and herself if her betrothal pact were broken.

Her mother, seeking ways to comfort her grieving daughter, could think only of what she had been taught many times during her own girlhood years.

"You are learning, my child, that a woman's fate is to taste bitterness. Yield, my dear one," she counseled. "Yield for the sake of family harmony."

Ahwa was too miserable to find solace in her mother's well-meant advice. She burst into tears.

Madam Shen sought once more to soothe Ahwa with words of time-worn wisdom.

"Learn from the willow tree. A mighty wind strikes the graceful willow tree. It bends to the onslaught, sways from side to side, but does not break. Like the majestic willow tree, it is better to accept what cannot be changed and by so doing spare one's self much unhappiness."

Old, painful memories came crowding out of Madam Shen's past as she witnessed her daughter's sorrow. From the time she had come to live in her husband's house, Madam Shen had borne her own private sadness with resignation. Shen Lingmou was a cruel, unfeeling man. Oh, the dreadful scenes when he had found fault with her and reviled her with curses! And the times when, sotted with drink, he had beaten her. The tears she had shed would have filled a rain barrel. Never could she reveal the hurt and shame to a soul.

Witnessing her daughter's anguish tore at Madam Shen's heart. For the first time, she decided on an act of defiance. By way of her old trusted servant, she sent a message to Yougwo.

"Ask the young man," she instructed, "to call on me before the week's end. Tell him that I regret his studies were interrupted by the flood. Let him know that I have the means to enable him to continue his education."

It was Madam Shen's hope that when her husband learned of Yougwo's renewed preparations for the civil service examinations, Shen would relent and permit Ahwa's marriage to take place as planned. Surely he would not reject a son-in-law who aspired to becoming a government official.

After she sent the servant off, Madam Shen wondered at her own daring. She would not permit herself to dwell on what might happen if her plan were to go awry. To bolster her confidence she disclosed her scheme to Ahwa, and while Ahwa shared her mother's misgivings, the very danger involved in taking so bold a step was also very exciting. Like two conspirators, they looked forward to Yougwo's visit.

The invitation from Madam Shen held out the promise of renewed hope for Yougwo. At the same time, it presented him with a problem. He had not a single presentable gown to wear. He would be mortified to enter the house of this kind lady dressed like a common beggar. How humiliating it would be to babble like a fool trying to apologize for his appearance. Still there might be a way out of his dilemma. He could arrange to borrow a gown from his wealthy cousin, Ren Yi.

Yougwo and his cousin were never close, being of opposite temperaments. Yougwo was a quiet, studious boy. His cousin early on had shown no interest in learning. Undisciplined by doting parents, Ren Yi grew up lacking in moral scruples. Even after he took a wife he did not discontinue his drinking and philandering. In fact, Ren Yi regarded Yougwo with scorn and ridiculed him for obediently and willingly shouldering his family duties with good cheer.

Yougwo saw Ren Yi rarely, only when family obligations demanded that they meet. The idea of asking his cousin for help made Yougwo extremely uncomfortable. Still, he saw no way to avoid it. Engrossed in his thoughts, he almost forgot that Madam Shen's servant was waiting patiently for his reply.

"Tell your mistress that I shall present myself at her house in three days."

In a hopeful mood, Yougwo went immediately to Ren Yi's residence. His optimism was soon dampened by a cold reception.

"You haven't shown your face around here for months. What brings you here now?"

"I've come to ask a special favor." Yougwo pretended not to take notice of the reproof. "I am to call on my future mother-in-law three days from now. She has made a kind offer of assistance that will enable me to complete my studies. I am ashamed to go dressed in old clothes. If you could lend me one of your gowns, I would be very grateful."

"Tell me about the girl you intend to marry." Ren Yi ignored Yougwo's request.

Anxious to please and win his cousin's help, Yougwo answered shyly.

"I am told she is very beautiful, so beautiful that blooming flowers close their petals and the moon hides behind a cloud at the sight of her face. Of course, I shall not see her until our wedding day, but the idea of setting foot in her house fills me with happy anticipation."

Ren Yi raised his eyebrows.

"Well, you are a lucky fellow," he remarked, but inwardly his

"Tell me about the girl you intend to marry."

thoughts were less pleasant. "This fool has managed to get himself a beautiful wife and wealthy in-laws besides. He deserves to have a few stumbling blocks thrown in his way." A rash scheme to scuttle Yougwo's plans was taking shape in Ren Yi's head. His tone became sweeter.

"Though you have shown up only because you are in need of a favor, I shall forgive you."

"Then you will agree to lend me some proper clothing?" Yougwo was greatly relieved.

"Yes, yes, but you shall have to be patient. I intend to visit an old friend. I shall return in time for you to keep your appointment. Until then, you can make up for your past discourtesy by remaining here. My mother spends much time alone and will be pleased to have your company."

On the appointed day for Yougwo's visit to the Shen home, it was Ren Yi who came instead. A maid showed him into the guest hall and asked that he wait until she could announce his arrival. At Madam Shen's entrance, Ren Yi bowed respectfully.

"You sent for me," he began. "I willingly accept your offer of help."

This young man has no manners, thought Madam Shen. Before uttering a word of polite conversation which good breeding dictates, he abruptly brings up my offer to assist him. She could not refrain from commenting about his poor taste.

"You are rather forward," she said. "Since you are a scholar, I would have expected you to be more reticent."

Ren Yi changed his tone. "I beg forgiveness. A poor man forgets the rules of polite conversation."

"I asked you to come," Madam Shen went on to explain, "because I wish to make it possible for you to continue your education. Money I cannot give you. However, I do have several pieces of valuable jewelry. The cash you will realize from their sale will amount to a fair sum."

"Such kindness is more than I deserve," said Ren Yi, with false humility.

"Then let us think only of your bright future," offered Madam Shen. She invited Ren Yi to stay for dinner and suggested he spend the night, since the hour was already late. To all her offers Ren Yi eagerly agreed. Little did Madam Shen suspect the sinister thoughts he harbored.

After they had eaten, Madam Shen excused herself, stating that she felt tired and wished to retire early. She asked the maid to show Ren Yi to the study where a bed would be made up for him, and she wished him a good night. Wide awake and alert, Ren Yi was feeling very pleased with his cleverness. He had managed to pass himself off as his cousin Yougwo. Madam Shen had been completely taken in by his ruse.

At last, all the house noises had subsided. Reasonably certain that everyone was asleep, Ren Yi made his way to Ahwa's room. He pushed gently against the door. It swung inward silently. Moonlight shone through a large window, outlining the form of the young girl asleep on her bed. A few quiet steps and he was at her side. He clamped his hand over her mouth.

"Do not cry out," he threatened. "Before long we will be married and share a bed. I heard tell of your radiant beauty, and I could not suppress my desire to be with you."

Immobilized by fear and confusion, the trembling Ahwa did not resist even when he undid her gown and forced his attentions upon her. Having satisfied his own base desires, he left the whimpering Ahwa without a backward glance.

Early the following morning, Ren Yi was taking leave of Madam Shen. She handed him a small embroidered string-tied purse and asked him to open it. His eyes were dazzled by the contents. She had given him three pieces of her most cherished jewelry: a gold pendant in the shape of a phoenix together with its heavy gold chain, a wide gold bracelet etched with a dragon design, and a priceless hair ornament set with hundreds of tiny pearls. Ren Yi understood that this generous gift was meant for Yougwo, yet he had not the slightest sense of guilt. On the contrary, he once again congratulated himself for his cunning. He had seduced his cousin's bride and had been handsomely rewarded by her mother.

Ahwa was left in a pitiable state after the shattering incident of the previous night. She had looked forward to marriage with eagerness. Appalled by her future husband's crude behavior, she now dreaded what lay ahead. If fate had intended for her a life of misery, she was powerless to challenge it. "Better to yield," her mother had instructed, and she decided to take the lesson to heart. Despite the unspeakable behavior of the man she was to marry, she would strive to be a dutiful wife. She dared to hope that her virtue would move him to show more tenderness, and with time he might even grow to love her.

An extraordinary visitor arrived at the Shen home the following day. He told an incredulous Madam Shen that he was Yougwo, her daughter's betrothed, and apologized for having come late in reply to her invitation. Too stunned to acknowledge his polite bow or return his greetings, Madam Chen was nevertheless favorably impressed by his appearance. He was impeccably dressed in a well-tailored, belted gown with ample sleeves piped in black silk. He was taller than average and quite handsome. His manners gave evidence of good breeding.

Yougwo detected that she seemed disturbed. He did not know what to make of it, nor could he understand why Madam Shen began to ply him with questions about his parents, the location of his family home, his father's occupation. He answered each query without the least hesitation, only adding to Madam Shen's bafflement.

Panic rose steadily in Madam Shen's chest. Her husband had spoken of Yougwo as a scholar. This young man's speech, polished manners and cordial demeanor confirmed that description. She had also been told of his good looks, and his youthful, pleasant face bore out that opinion as well.

"Who delivered my invitation to you?" asked Madam Shen, hoping to catch him in a lie.

"An elderly servant who walked with the aid of a cane," he replied directly.

"The description fits," thought Madam Shen, growing ever more confused. She leaned back in her chair and put her hands over her eyes. She was searching for something to say while

Yougwo, bewildered and unable to comprehend why he was being grilled, waited for an explanation.

By now, Madam Shen was reasonably certain that Yougwo was her daughter's legitimate suitor. But she could not tell him about the events of the previous day without revealing that she had been duped by an unknown imposter. Stalling for time, she called for the maid.

"I have asked our visitor to join me in taking some refreshment. Prepare two bowls of lotus seed sweet soup, rice cakes, and tea," she directed.

While waiting for the maid to return, Madam Shen inquired about Yougwo's plans for the future. He had to postpone sitting for the civil service examinations, he told her, because his father could not afford traveling expenses to send him to the capital.

"I will find a way," he said, "for I am determined to succeed."

Madam Shen admired his courage and vaguely spoke of helping him at some future date. Her jewelry gone, she could offer him nothing at the moment, and it saddened her.

Within a short while, the maid reappeared carrying a large tray. She set the tray down on a low table. From a porcelain tureen she filled two bowls with steaming soup, set out the rice cakes, bowed, and left. Madam Shen and Yougwo began to sip the fragrant broth. Both felt uneasy, she harboring worrisome misgivings about the results of her meddling, he wondering why he had been invited at all.

All at once they heard a high-pitched scream, then the sound of running feet. The maid burst in, wailing, "Come quickly, something dreadful has happened!" Madam Shen and Yougwo followed at her heels to Ahwa's room. Hanging from a beam by a noose fashioned out of a sash was Ahwa's lifeless body. Madam Shen swooned and sank to the floor.

Yougwo remained discreetly behind a screen while servants cut Ahwa loose and carried her to her bed.

When Madam Shen came to in her own chamber, the maid was straightening the bed covers and plumping the pillows. Gradually, as her mind cleared, Madam Shen was struck anew by the horror of what had happened. Burying her head in the pil-

Yougwo remained discreetly behind a screen
while servants carried Ahwa to her bed.

lows, she ignored the tender ministrations of her worried maid. The devoted servant bent close to her mistress.

"The young man has not left," she whispered. "He has been waiting for you to recover. He wishes to offer you his condolences." Madam Shen shook her head. She wanted to be alone with her sorrow.

"I have found this," the maid continued offering her mistress a slip of paper. Madam Shen at once recognized her daughter's handwriting.

"My dear wronged child," she moaned. She motioned to the maid to summon Yougwo. When he entered the room, Madam Shen, her composure restored, held out the note and requested that he read it to her.

In a subdued voice, Yougwo read, "'I greet you with love, mother, and ask forgiveness. I overheard your conversation with my intended husband, Yougwo. I now know that the evil man who last night entered my room and stripped me of my virtue was a pretender. Please understand that I had no choice but to depart this earth. In the next life, if it is destined, Yougwo and I shall meet again. Offer him my gold bracelet as a gift of remembrance. In heaven, my prayers will be for your health and long life. Do not grieve for your unworthy daughter, Ahwa.' "

Oh, the unbearable sorrow! Madam Shen rocked back and forth, clutching her head to still the pounding. A crushing sense of guilt added to her anguish. How could she face her husband? To disclose the truth would send him into a raving tantrum. She tore Ahwa's note to pieces and asked the maid to throw the bits of paper into the fire. Now she would have to concoct some reasonable explanation for the tragedy that had befallen her family.

Shen returned from his business trip earlier than expected. The servant who let him in kept her eyes cast downward, bowed, and quickly hurried off. Neither Madam Shen nor Ahwa appeared to welcome him back.

Removing his outer garment, he called out, "Are there no others here? Am I to be greeted only by silent ghosts?" The maid reappeared.

"Madam Shen is not feeling well," she said in a faint voice. "She is resting in her bedchamber."

"And where is my daughter?" The maid fled, trying to stifle a sob.

Shen went quickly to his wife's side, fearing she had fallen gravely ill during his absence. His appearance sent Madam Shen into a fit of moaning such as he had never heard before.

"What is the matter?" Shen asked, but he was sure his wife had not heard him, for she continued to groan and rave.

"Ay, ay, our daughter no longer walks upon the earth. Her soul wanders toward the heavenly kingdom."

"What are you saying?" demanded Shen, grabbing the crazed woman by the shoulders.

"How did it happen? When? Speak!"

There was no escaping the inevitable confrontation Madam Shen had so dreaded. She would have to tell him the flimsy tale she had rehearsed and hope that he would not see through the deception.

"While you were gone, Ahwa's suitor, Yougwo, came to pay his respects. He seemed such an amiable young man, soft-spoken, courteous. He talked seriously about his studies and his hopes for the future. He told me he had completed his studies and had found the means to travel to the capital for the civil service examinations. I really grew to like him and invited him to stay for the night since the hour was late. What a fool I was not to see beyond his false show of civility! When everyone was asleep, he stole into Ahwa's room, worse still, into her bed, to satisfy his evil desires. The next day the dear girl was too ashamed to speak of it. I managed to gain her confidence and she revealed what had happened."

Grim-faced, Shen started to pace back and forth, his lips drawn tight, his eyes flashing anger.

"My innocent child," Madam Shen quickly continued, hoping to forestall her husband's wrathful outburst. "I could not console her. I never suspected her grief would so overwhelm her that she would take her life."

Madam Shen lay back on the pillows, eyes shut. To her surprise Shen remained silent. Turning away from her he stalked out, muttering to himself.

The day after Ahwa's funeral, Shen delivered a petition to Lord Bau, claiming that Yougwo was responsible for his daughter's death and demanding that justice be done.

Shen's complaint was not the only thing Lord Bau had to consider. He had also received word from Madam Shen.

"What am I to make of this?" Lord Bau mused. "A father accuses a young man of causing his daughter's death. Then the mother sends me an urgent plea to spare the accused, declaring he is without fault."

On many previous occasions, Lord Bau had been called upon to settle family disputes. This case, however, involving the death of a blameless girl, was more serious. He wished first to question the girl's mother and sent his aides to escort Madam Shen to the *yamen*.

Madam Shen, caught in her own web of lies, knew that in the presence of Lord Bau she could not dissemble. The time for deceit was over. The possibility that Yougwo, who had done no wrong, could face execution as a result of her falsehood, plunged her into even greater despair. Haltingly, she recounted exactly what had preceded Ahwa's suicide.

"My only desire was to ensure my daughter's happiness. Please," she begged, "let me not be the cause of yet another death."

"I shall carefully consider what you have told me," Lord Bau assured her. "Nevertheless, you must understand that I cannot rely solely on your word. It will be necessary to make further investigations. In the meantime, do not repeat to anyone what you have divulged to me. We shall try to establish the identity of the man who posed as your daughter's betrothed."

When it was his time to be questioned by Lord Bau, Yougwo also seemed incapable of shedding any light on the identity of the impostor. Nervous and shy, he was still despondent over the tragedy of Ahwa's suicide. Even more devastating was the accusation that he was the cause of her death. Sensing his discomfort, Lord Bau probed carefully. He asked Yougwo to recall as best he could what had occurred prior to his arrival at Madam Shen's house.

Yougwo flushed with embarrassment having to reveal how his ill-natured cousin had berated him.

"My cousin finally agreed to lend me a gown," he added, "on condition that I keep his mother company while he left to visit a friend. He detained me for three days so that I was late in keeping my appointment with my future mother-in-law."

Lord Bau's interest quickened. His questions became more pointed.

"How old is your cousin?"

"We were born in the same year of the dragon, sir."

"Where does your cousin reside?"

"In the village of Lwomaying, with his aged mother. When his father died, my cousin Ren Yi became the head of the household and took over the family's porcelain business."

"One last question," said Lord Bau. "You tell me that your cousin deals in porcelains. Does he manufacture tableware or does he sell expensive antique pieces?"

This seemed a strange thing to ask, Yougwo thought, but he answered directly.

"My cousin does both. He has a reputation for being a shrewd businessman."

"That will be all for now," concluded Lord Bau.

Alone in the quiet of his office, Lord Bau considered several ways he might develop an ironclad case against Ren Yi. The scheme he finally decided upon involved a good deal of play-acting. He would call on Ren Yi disguised as a porcelain merchant.

To prepare for the visit, Lord Bau asked his wife to wrap a set of her highest quality bowls in several layers of soft cotton cloth. Then he placed the delicate pieces in a woven straw basket. Attired in the guise of a merchant, he appeared at Ren Yi's house.

Never one to turn down a good business deal, Ren Yi was interested in buying the bowls Lord Bau offered for sale. He recognized that they were of a superior design and that the price was attractive. Mentally he calculated the profit they would bring when resold. But having recently lost heavily at the gaming tables, he did not have enough money to pay for them.

"Will you sell me just one of the bowls?" he asked. "I find myself a little short of cash at the moment."

"I cannot break up a set," Lord Bau told him. "However, I see that you are a good judge of value and I like to deal with people who appreciate excellent quality. If you take all three bowls, I am willing to reduce the asking price by one third."

"What an exceptional offer!" thought Ren Yi. Buy cheap, sell dear, was the rule he worked by, and it disturbed him that he might lose out on making a handsome profit.

Lord Bau sensed the greediness his last offer had stirred up in Ren Yi.

"It's too bad that you are without money," he remarked, "but I am not a hard-hearted man. If you have other effects of value— paintings, perhaps, or some jewelry—I am willing to accept those items in lieu of cash."

Ren Yi jumped at the chance. Excusing himself, he left the room and returned in a few moments with a silk purse. He loosened the drawstring and took out three pieces of jewelry: a gold pendant in the shape of a phoenix together with its heavy gold chain, a wide gold bracelet etched with a dragon design, and a hair ornament inset with hundreds of tiny pearls.

Lord Bau made a pretense of examining them closely, turning them over and over in his hand as though he were appraising their worth.

"Well," he announced to Ren Yi's relief, "they are not of the best quality, but I'll take them anyway."

With Madam Shen's jewels safely in his possession, Lord Bau took his leave. At a discreet distance, his two aides awaited his signal. They moved to carry out their master's orders.

Ren Yi was beaming with satisfaction over his clever purchase when there was a knock at the door. Upon raising the latch, he was confronted by Lord Bau's aides. They grabbed him and hauled him off to the *yamen*. Thrust before Lord Bau, Ren Yi knew at once that he had been outsmarted, that his treachery had been discovered. There, behind his large desk, sat Lord Bau, stern and unsmiling. Standing off to one side, Ren Yi saw Shen and his wife. At Lord Bau's elbow lay the string purse, which Ren Yi recognized immediately.

Lord Bau extracted the contents of the purse piece by piece and laid them on his desk for all to see.

"Can you identify these pieces of jewelry?" he asked, addressing Madam Shen.

Pointing an accusing finger at Ren Yi, she declared without hesitation, "These are the same jewels I gave this man, because he fooled me into believing that he was my future son-in-law."

"Do you deny it?" Lord Bau demanded of Ren Yi severely. Ren Yi made no reply. "I take your silence to be an admission of guilt," declared Lord Bau. "I now charge you with causing the death of Shen Lingmou's daughter."

"Death? Your Honor, you accuse me of a crime I did not commit."

Without showing any sign of contrition, Ren Yi tried to wheedle his way out of his predicament. Appealing to Lord Bau, he argued, "I do admit to forcing my way into the girl's bed. I only meant to indulge my natural appetite for a pretty female who enticed me with her beauty. She was very much alive when I left her. It is an outright lie to say that I was in any way responsible for her death."

"So now we add another charge, rape!" bellowed Lord Bau. "Guilty, guilty, on all counts. The penalty is death by beheading."

But even as Ren Li was being led away, Lord Bau felt a twinge of uneasiness. To sentence a man to death weighed heavily on his conscience. Though the scoundrel deserved the severe judgment, a portion of blame lay elsewhere.

Addressing Shen, he said, "You are not without blame in this unfortunate situation. If you had not threatened to violate the social order by breaking a sacred agreement, your daughter would be alive today. What needless suffering you have brought upon yourself and others by your folly."

It had never occurred to Shen that he bore the slightest responsibility. Lord Bau's words sobered him and he accepted the reprimand humbly. Shen could not restore Ahwa to life, but he honored the betrothal agreement by adopting Yougwo as his own son.

Madam Shen was pleased. She had a few thoughts of her own. Like her husband, she longed to salvage some good from the tragedy. This time she would not act without consulting Shen.

"Ren Yi's wife is left a widow," she pointed out. "Yougwo is left without a bride. How splendid it would be to arrange a marriage between them! This way we shall gain a daughter as well as a son."

Shen willingly agreed. As the years passed, the pain of Ahwa's death was softened by the birth of many grandchildren.

A Bloody Handprint

Chen Ching mournfully concluded that all the demons of hell had chosen him to be the victim of some devilish prank. How else explain why he was at this moment sitting on the cold stone floor of a foul-smelling prison cell, accused of murdering a holy monk? He tried to turn his head slightly and winced with pain. Because he had dared to protest his innocence while the brutish jailers fumbled clumsily to clamp the *cangue** around his neck, he had been cruelly beaten. The purple welts raised by their bamboo rods stung painfully and the wooden collar threatened to choke him. To avoid further agony he forced himself to sit perfectly still. But while his body remained motionless, his mind raced along a thousand paths of remembrance.

Chen recalled leaving his home in high spirits in anticipation of a happy reunion with an old friend. His journey took him a short distance over a well-traveled route before he veered off to a quiet lane that twisted and turned, climbing steadily into the hills. Passing a clump of stunted pines, Chen noticed a weather-beaten wooden tablet with the words TEMPLE OF HEAVENLY LIGHT scratched into its surface. He gave it only a fleeting glance. The weather was pleasant. It was early spring, neither too warm nor too cold, and he continued to stride along briskly.

---

*A wooden collar which confines the neck, and sometimes the hands, used for punishment.

Without incident, Chen reached his friend's house just as the first star appeared in the darkening sky. Sitting down to dine at a table heaped with bowls of steaming noodles, delicately fried pork, and a large platter of richly spiced stir-fried vegetables, both men savored the tasty food and chatted amiably. They had not seen each other for almost a year and there was much to talk about. The warm wine they sipped during the meal made Chen drowsy. Shown to the guest room in the western wing, he fell asleep almost immediately beneath the warm, quilted covers.

The next few days passed quickly. When the hour of Chen's departure arrived, the old companions dawdled over the morning meal in an effort to delay the moment of leave-taking. By the time Chen waved his last farewell at the end of the path leading from his friend's house to the public road, the sun was already directly overhead.

The return journey proved to be more arduous. It had turned warmer. By early afternoon, dark clouds had moved in. Chen heard the distant rumble of thunder. He welcomed the first cool raindrops.

A passing shower, he thought. Just a harmless sprinkle. But the heavens suddenly opened, releasing a drenching downpour and dampening his optimism. Before long he was soaked clear through to the skin. The dusty road eagerly drank up the water until it could hold no more. Globs of sticky mud clung to Chen's sandals, making every step an effort, while the heavy drops pelted him without pause.

Across the open fields, as far as he could see, there was not a single house. Chen trudged on, head bent against the wind. His face lit up when once again he came upon the tablet with its inscription, TEMPLE OF HEAVENLY LIGHT, a perfect place to wait out the storm. Chen felt certain that the monks who lived there would welcome a weary traveler, even provide him with a night's lodging.

It was still raining steadily. He lifted the knocker of the temple door and struck it several times, expecting someone to respond. While waiting, he had time to observe that the grounds around the temple were suffering from long neglect. What may formerly have been well-tended gardens had become weed-choked patches. As for the temple walls, they, too, had deteriorated badly. Many of the roof tiles had fallen off and lay scattered all about.

Chen raised the knocker once more, striking it harder and longer. No one came. With some trepidation he gently pushed the door open. Aside from the creaky hinges, he heard not a sound. It took a moment for his eyes to become adjusted to the dimness of the interior before he could make out a deep cavernous room. His curiosity overcame his caution, and he stepped inside.

At the far end of the long hall, a great smiling Buddha reclined cross-legged atop a high platform. At either side of the corpulent Buddha stood two fierce, giant-size figures, guardians of the temple. Their grotesque faces, designed to frighten away evil spirits, gave Chen a start. All the statues were in a miserable state of disrepair. The gold leaf was peeling from their arms and legs; fine cracks crisscrossed their entire bodies. The venerated Buddha had lost an ear, and his nose was chipped.

Why had this house of worship been forsaken? Where had the saffron-robed monks gone? Perhaps their ghosts still dwelt among the rafters or crouched in hidden niches. Frightened, Chen started to back away, having decided that he could not rest easily in this haunted place.

A blinding flash of lightning, followed by an instant clap of thunder, made him reconsider. He stood just inside the doorway of the ruined temple, listening to the rain beat down on the tile roof in a rhythmic tattoo, and waited. When the storm showed no sign of letting up, Chen thought it wiser to risk the company of ghosts rather than brave the unfriendly elements.

With apprehension, he approached the platform. He bowed respectfully before each of the five statues, then cautiously bedded down on the earthen floor in front of the great Buddha, hoping that in the presence of the most revered of sages he would be protected from harm.

He awoke to the pale light of dawn peeping through a crack in the roof. He was hungry, having had nothing to eat since early the day before. His mouth felt dry and sour. Rising to his feet, he began to straighten his rumpled gown. It seemed odd that it had dried in front, though the back still felt damp.

Chen walked quickly to the main road. The storm had passed during the night, leaving the air fresh and clean. He expected to reach his village before day's end.

He could not have taken more than a hundred paces before he heard someone bark a command.

"Halt!" Chen turned to see where the voice was coming from, never suspecting that the order was addressed to him.

"Do not take another step or you will have cause to regret it." Chen froze on the spot.

"The back of your gown is stained with blood. What have you been up to?" asked the watch who was patrolling the area.

"Stained with blood?" Chen repeated with a puzzled look.

"You blackguards are all the same," growled the watch. "When caught red-handed you always feign ignorance." In an iron grip the watch held on to Chen's arm. "What is your name? Where are you from? What is your destination?"

Chen answered honestly. "My name is Chen Ching. I reside in Ding Syan. Last night I was caught in a rainstorm and sought shelter in the Temple Of Heavenly Light."

"How do you account for the blood on your gown?" the watch persisted.

"If there is blood on my gown, sir, I do not know how it came to be there. I was drenched when I reached the temple. Tired and footsore, I lay down in front of the big Buddha. When I awoke at dawn, I hastened to leave the temple, eager to return home without further delay."

"Scoundrel, do you take me for a fool? Return to the temple with me!"

Never relinquishing his hold on Chen's arm, the watch hurried him back over the temple path and pushed him roughly through the door.

"Now, show me where you say you slept," he demanded.

Chen pointed toward the spot below the platform. Then the

watch dragged Chen behind the statue. There, lying face up, a knife embedded in his chest, was the body of a dead monk.

"You are under arrest," the watch declared.

To add to Chen's misfortune, Lord Bau, who ordinarily would have heard his case promptly, was away. The wise judge had been summoned by the emperor to counsel his majesty on a grave matter of state. Cases were being held up until the judge's return. Along with other prisoners, Chen languished in jail. He had plenty of time to bemoan his fate and despaired that he could ever extricate himself from this twisted knot of circumstances.

An entire month passed before Lord Bau was ready to take up his normal duties. He was eager to clear up the backlog of work that had accumulated in his absence.

"You have just returned from the long trip to the capital. Why not rest a day or two?" suggested Lord Bau's closest aide, Bau Sying.

"There will be plenty of time to rest when one is laid in the grave," Lord Bau retorted, busying himself with a pile of papers on his desk. "Bring in the prisoner who has been held the longest."

Lord Bau looked up from his papers only when the door opened and Chen was led in. The guard removed the *cangue*.

"Kneel," he commanded, pushing down on Chen's shoulder with a heavy hand. Chen sank to his knees, but the overzealous guard was not satisfied.

"Head down!" he shouted, bending Chen's head forward so he could not look directly at Lord Bau.

Lord Bau estimated the age of the prisoner to be about thirty. He was short and very slight of build, hardly the kind of man who could easily overpower someone and stab him to death. Having read the complaint filed by the watch, other doubts about Chen's guilt occurred to Lord Bau, but he would keep them in abeyance for now.

"Did you kill the monk as you are charged?" asked Lord Bau. Chen raised his head to answer. In a flash, the guard was upon him. Chen thought his neck would snap, so fiercely was his head shoved down.

"Honorable Master, I have never hurt a single soul, never." Chen spoke with a quavering voice, not daring to look up.

"If you have done nothing wrong, why are you here?"

"I cannot say, Honorable Judge, other than that I have been mistakenly accused. I only know I am innocent of any crime, and I humbly beg Your Honor for justice."

"Stand," directed Lord Bau. Chen did as he was ordered.

"I will listen to your account of what happened," offered Lord Bau, "but speak quickly and to the point. I do not have time to waste."

Encouraged by Lord Bau's willingness to hear his version of the perplexing events, Chen began.

"I am Chen Ching of Ding Syan village. While traveling, I was caught in a rainstorm. I spent the night in the abandoned Temple of Heavenly Light." Chen went on to tell why the watch had accused him of murdering the monk. "Please, Your Honor," Chen implored, "I swear that I did not kill him nor do I have any idea who did." Chen was out of breath. He sucked in a long draft of air and fell silent.

"Take the prisoner back to his cell," Lord Bau instructed the guard.

Chen was led away wondering why he had not been set free. He had heard tell that Lord Bau could determine a man's innocence just by looking at him. Surely Lord Bau should have seen that his was not the face of a murderer.

The cell door slammed shut with a loud clang. Chen felt more wretched than ever, tortured by the grim thought that though he had done no wrong, he remained accused of taking another's life. He pictured his neck under the executioner's blade. Had Chen been able to fathom Lord Bau's mind, he would not have so easily given up hope, for Lord Bau had all but concluded that Chen was not implicated in the monk's death.

Lord Bau sat at his desk, lost in contemplation. One question troubled him in particular. If Chen Ching had killed the monk by stabbing him in the chest with a long knife, the blood spurting from the wound would have landed on the front of Chen's gown.

The only visible bloodstain was on the upper back of his garment.

"I would like to examine the scene of the crime myself," Lord Bau announced. "Prepare to accompany me." His aide acknowledged his comments with a nod of the head.

All along the way to the temple, Lord Bau mulled over Chen's recital of how he had been taken into custody. The location of the bloodstain continued to nag at him, and he became irritable, for he was accustomed to finding solutions easily.

"Must you shake this sedan chair so violently," he bellowed from within its curtained privacy. The sweating carriers slowed their pace to please their eminent passenger.

Once inside the temple, Lord Bau remained keenly alert to anything that might prove significant to his investigation. He approached the statues with reverence, and bowed. He noticed a deep red circular stain on the ground in front of the platform. Making a mental note of the observation, he slowly walked to the rear. There he found another similarly discolored patch on the ground, this one larger than the first.

Lord Bau then shifted his attention to the great Buddha's back. There was a peculiar set of markings below the right shoulder. It appeared to be a handprint. Stranger still, the hand that had made the print had six fingers, an extra digit between the thumb and forefinger. Lord Bau stepped forward to examine the fascinating discovery more closely. Continuing to circle the statue, his foot struck a small object. Glancing down, he saw it was a carpenter's ink marker. He retrieved it and tucked it into his wide sleeve. At last, the clues were beginning to fall into place.

The unfortunate monk had lost a great deal of blood when he was stabbed and left lying behind the Buddha. His life's fluid had seeped under the platform to the very spot where Chen's back had rested while he slept. It was now obvious why only the back of Chen's gown was stained with blood. So far, so good. But the motive for the killing still was clouded in mystery. And even more baffling was the extraordinary hand print.

"I have seen all that I wish to see," Lord Bau told his aide.

"As you say, Master. Your Lordship must indeed be weary

Once inside the temple, Lord Bau remained keenly alert to
anything that might prove significant to his investigation.

and in need of a rest. In truth, if I may be so bold as to offer an opinion, your work schedule would exhaust a younger and stronger man."

"Nonsense!" retorted Lord Bau. "It is only the lazy shirker who regards honest labor as excessive. Besides, a man rots in a foul cell accused of a crime I believe he did not commit."

Back in his office, Lord Bau asked Sying to make a list of all the carpenters in Ding County. "Inform them that upon my orders they are to appear before me at noon tomorrow." Lest he provoke another reprimand, Sying deemed it wiser to refrain from commenting about this singular request.

The next day, nine professional carpenters assembled in the great hall of the *yamen*. They were greeted personally by Lord Bau.

"I have called you here because I would like to have some special stands built to hold my flowering plants. Horticulture is one of my hobbies, and I enjoy displaying the flowers in a way that enhances their beauty. Therefore, I ask each of you to design a decorative stand that will serve that purpose. Consider this a contest to demonstrate your individual talents. The one who creates the design I prefer above all the others will be handsomely rewarded."

Tables were set up, paper, ink stones, and brushes distributed, and the carpenters set to work. Lord Bau walked quietly among them, glancing over their shoulders, paying particular attention to their hands. When all had at last put down their brushes, Lord Bau examined the designs one by one. As he went from table to table, the carpenters watched for a sign of approval. They might as well have been watching a blank wall, for he remained expressionless. The contestants grew tense.

"What is your name?" asked Lord Bau casually when he came to the last man.

"I am Wu Liang, Honorable Master."

"Remain here. I would like to have a word with you." Lord Bau thanked the other carpenters for their work, paid them each a modest sum, and dismissed them.

Wu Liang wore a wide smile as they filed out of the room. It was not only pride in his work that made him beam with delight.

Tables were set up, paper, ink stones, and brushes
distributed, and carpenters set to work.

He was thinking of the reward, which he hoped would be generous.

"Have you ever been to the Temple of Heavenly Light?" inquired Lord Bau.

The carpenter paled. His grin melted away.

"I have not been there for a long time."

"When were you last there?"

"I do not recall."

"Was not your most recent visit made on a day before a heavy rainstorm?"

Wu Liang swallowed. He did not respond.

"On that particular day, a holy monk was stabbed to death behind the statue of the great Buddha. You are the murderer, Wu Liang!"

A look of terror crept over Wu Liang's face.

"Honorable Master, I am a lowly carpenter. I have no reason to murder a monk. How can you suspect me of such a heinous act?"

"I have learned from the Buddha himself that you are the killer."

The shocked Wu Liang began to stammer a denial. Though shaken, he clung doggedly to his claim of innocence. "Statues do not speak," thought Wu Liang, "and the judge knows that as well as I do. He thinks I am a superstitious oaf and he is just trying to trick me into a confession."

"Very well," countered Wu Liang, "if the Buddha accuses me, let him do so in my presence."

"You shall have your wish tomorrow when your case is heard in court," agreed Lord Bau, taking up Wu Liang's bluff.

The following morning, Wu Liang was escorted into the courtroom by two guards. The hall was filled with curious onlookers. Wu Liang felt as if a thousand piercing eyes were following him. Directly behind the judge loomed a large object draped in white cloth.

With the striking of a gong, a hush fell over the room. A court attendant unfurled a tightly rolled scroll and read out the formal charges against the accused.

"Wu Liang," boomed Lord Bau's voice, "you have heard the charges against you. How do you plead?"

"I am an innocent man," cried Wu Liang.

"Consider carefully what you say," warned Lord Bau. "You asked to confront your accuser face to face. He is at this very moment in your presence and eager to meet you." With this, the court attendant pulled the white cloth from the large object behind Lord Bau. There sat the great Buddha of the Temple of Heavenly Light, lips parted in a smile, enormous round belly hanging over his crossed legs. Wu Liang felt as though he had been dealt a hammer blow.

"Before the witness exposes your treachery, Wu Liang, do you wish to reconsider and confess?"

Stunned, Wu Liang nevertheless managed not to lose control. "Ay," he groaned. "Some kind of trap has been laid, and if I am not careful I shall fall into it. But I am no fool. If I hold my ground I may not get caught."

"I have done no wrong," he insisted arrogantly.

"Very well, then, I must call upon the witness." At an almost imperceptible signal from Lord Bau, the two court attendants turned the statue of the great Buddha around so that his back was visible to all.

"Wu Liang, do you see a handprint on the right shoulder blade of the Buddha?"

Wu Liang's tongue clung to his palate. He uttered not a sound.

"That print was made by a hand covered with blood."

"What has that to do with me?" shouted Wu Liang, surprising himself with his own audacity.

"The hand that made the print was not an ordinary hand. It has six fingers. Hold up your left hand, Wu Liang."

Wu kept his arms glued to his sides. Before he knew what was happening, an attendant grasped his left hand and raised it high above his head. Plainly evident was the extra digit between the thumb and forefinger! From the spectators a murmur arose that grew to a threatening roar.

"He has six fingers, confess, confess, murderer, villain, beast!"

"Out with it," demanded Lord Bau. "Why did you kill the holy monk?"

Stubbornly, Wu Liang refused to yield. A masked guard

moved toward him with a stout bamboo rod in his hand. Wu deemed it wiser to save himself from the torture of a beating.

"I am guilty," he sobbed. "Have pity, Honorable Master. Strong drink addled my brain and turned me from a peaceful man into a demon."

Shorn of all bravado, Wu Liang recounted what had taken place on that fateful day in the Temple of Heavenly Light.

"The monk was my best friend. He lived alone in the broken-down ruins of the temple. Often he invited me to spend a few hours with him because he was lonely. On the day of my last visit, we were sitting on the ground behind the Buddha, drinking heavily. I matched him cup for cup of good wine. When the hour grew late, I made ready to leave. We were both happily drunk, and he clung to me, begging me to stay on. His foul breath was nauseating.

" 'Why don't you find a disciple to keep you company?' I asked, pushing him away and holding him at arm's length. 'You are growing older. You will need someone to look after you.' My friend shook his head.

" 'An honest disciple is hard to find. He will rob me of the full purse of money I have put aside for my old age.'

"I thought he was bragging. I asked him where he kept ·so much money.

" 'Come closer.' He spoke in a hoarse whisper. 'No one knows where it is hidden. With you, my dear and devoted friend, I shall share my secret. The great Buddha's head is hollow. I have stashed a goodly sum there by cutting an opening behind the right ear. Who will ever think to look there? Pretty clever,' the self-satisfied monk boasted.

"Saliva drooled from his mouth and ran down his chin. It was disgusting for me to look at him. He passed out and lay motionless, arms and legs outstretched. My head cleared, and I remained there listening to his loud snoring.

"Of a sudden, an evil demon took hold of my soul. This impious monk will soon drink himself to death. The signs are already apparent, inflamed eyes, a red, bulbous nose, dry, jaundiced skin.

When he dies, all the money he has accumulated will be left to rot in the Buddha's head. Worse still, a thief may ransack the temple and carry it off. Better that his fortune fall into my hands. Yet, if I take his money, I would betray an old friend who has confided in me. Thus a battle raged in my head and in my heart, a battle between sentiment and common sense. In the end, common sense won.

"I climbed onto the platform. The Buddha's statue was huge and I considered how best to reach the head. Just then my befuddled friend stirred and called out. 'Where are you?'

"Without hesitation, I ran to his living quarters and found a knife. I crouched beside him with my hand upraised, ready to plunge it into his breast. Suddenly, he sat up. Through glazed eyes he regarded me with disbelief. One well-aimed thrust and his life was at an end."

"Let me finish your tale," interrupted Lord Bau. "Much blood flowed from the wound, staining your clothes and covering your hands. So eager were you to find the money you did not stop to clean yourself. Bespattered with blood, you climbed onto the platform, stood on the Buddha's belly, and holding onto his back with your left hand, you reached for the hole behind his ear. Your bloodied hand made a perfect print!"

Lord Bau withdrew from his wide sleeve a carpenter's ink marker. "Does this belong to you?" He held it out for Wu Liang to examine it.

At a loss as to how his ink marker had come into Lord Bau's possession, Wu Liang acknowledged that it was his.

"I found it on the floor of the temple," Lord Bau pressed on. "You must have dropped it while fighting with your friend. Like most criminals, you believed you would never be found out because there were no witnesses. Dolt that you are, you left not only one witness but two, albeit both were silent. They gave undeniable testimony against you. The handprint on the Buddha's back was the first witness. Your carpenter's ink marker was the second. It revealed your trade."

Wu Liang knew that his fate was sealed, that his own life

would soon be at an end. Strangely enough, he remained calm at this moment of truth, relieved that his agony was over.

"My Lord," he said, bowing respectfully from the waist, "you are the wisest among men." These were the last words Wu Liang ever uttered.

Immediately following Wu Liang's conviction, Chen Ching was released. Lord Bau sent him away with an expression of regret for his suffering and a modest sum of money as compensation for his undeserved imprisonment. For many years thereafter, Chen Ching never tired of telling how his life had been spared due to the intervention of the wise Lord Bau.

Singsong Girl

Early on a misty morning of the third day of the third month, Shanji and his wife were climbing the steep path that led to the ancestral graveyard. They were making their journey to pay homage to Shanji's mother, whose soul had departed on its journey to the Yellow Springs less than a year ago.

From a pole slung across Shanji's shoulders dangled a double-layered basket. Each layer contained two bowls of freshly prepared delicacies, red-cooked duck, sliced chicken, sweet and sour pork, and seaweed pastries. Following close behind him, his wife held incense and paper money in one hand, and a pitcher filled with wine in the other. Fingers of fog creeping down from the mountain peaks enveloped them. Adding to their discomfort, droplets of rain began to fall from the low-hanging clouds.

Shanji's disagreeable thoughts matched the worsening weather. Instead of focusing his mind on his deceased mother, he was silently venting his fury on his very much alive elderly father. So absorbed was he that he remained unmindful of the chilling drizzle.

"Shanji, I cannot keep up with you!" he heard his lagging wife complain. "And if I hurry I shall spill the wine."

Shanji did not bother to answer. Impatient to reach his destination, he lengthened his strides. His wife would have to fend for herself. The hard-packed earthen path had become slippery, but Shanji took no notice. The moment he arrived at his mother's gravesite he hurriedly unloaded the baskets and placed them on the stone table in front of his mother's memorial tablet. His brow furrowed with anxiety, he did not wait for his wife but knelt down and rested his forehead against the stone marker. Surely his mother's spirit would be sympathetic to his complaints and restore to his soul a measure of tranquility.

"Honorable Mother," Shanji began reverently, "I beg your forgiveness, for I have disturbed your eternal rest, but perhaps you can help me find a way to change the reprehensible behavior of my aged father. On this sacred day of the tomb festival he is not with me . . . "

Interrupting his train of thought, his wife, now standing beside him, burst out, "Shanji, in my haste to catch up with you I tripped and spilled some of the wine. I hope our dear mother will not be offended."

Already in a foul mood, Shanji was further irritated by his wife's clumsiness. He turned toward her and lashed out, "You worthless fool! You have never given me a moment's pleasure."

Shanji's wife kept her silence. She did not wish to rile him, for when his temper flared he would curse her for her barren womb. From the half-empty pitcher she poured several small bowls of wine and arranged them on the stone table. Quietly, she knelt beside him.

With great effort, Shanji controlled his agitation and continued to address his departed mother.

"Instead of accompanying us on this visit to your grave, father has gone to a brothel to seek out his favorite singsong girl. The gods have given him the gift of long life. This month he will attain the venerable age of eighty years. His beard is white, his eyesight poor, and he walks with the aid of a cane. His visits to the brothel have made him the laughingstock of the village. I have tried to reason with him, but he will not listen. Whenever my wife and I call on him, he is not there to receive us, for he is off carousing with his singsong girl. Mother, I realize I am not a perfect son. Gambling is my weakness. In the past I have won as much as I have lost, but recently my luck has run out. I am deeply in debt. My friends are clamoring for their money. I am my father's only son and sole heir, yet he refuses my pleas for help. Instead, he is squandering my inheritance on jewels and baubles for a good-for-nothing harlot." Shanji had bared his heart. With his head pressed to the cold tombstone, he felt a measure of consolation.

The rain had ceased but not before it had soaked through his jacket. Uncomfortable and cold, Shanji rose and motioned to his wife that he was ready to leave. She dutifully burned the paper money, put the food back into the basket, and followed him down the sloping path. A brisk breeze began to whisk away the grey clouds. The sun broke through the patchwork sky. Shanji's gloom fell away and he dared to hope that his father would abandon his foolishness and come to his senses.

Shanji's good feeling lasted only until he neared the entrance gate of the family compound. Runners carrying his father's sedan chair were approaching from the opposite direction. When they reached the gate they set the chair down and helped the old man descend. From a second chair a slender young girl emerged. She wore a deep red cape caught at the collar by a jeweled clasp. Her thick hair, piled on the top of her head, was held by two gem-encrusted combs, and her silver earrings jangled with a musical tinkle as she moved past Shanji. Shanji glimpsed her heavily painted face and was overcome with revulsion. How dare his father bring a singsong girl home from the brothel! While she lives in luxury, I, his own son, must scramble to make ends meet. It is an outrage!

Unaware of Shanji's hostility, Meimei, smiling happily, passed through the ornate gate. Awed by the blue-green tile roof with brightly colored dragons and scaly fish decorating its eaves and ridges, she was even more impressed when she stepped inside the house. In the center of the main hall stood a heavy table, its red wood polished to a high gloss. Placed at each end were tall blue and white porcelain vases filled with bouquets of freshly cut peach blossoms. Exquisitely painted scrolls depicting tree-clad mountains, winding rivers and cascading waterfalls decorated the walls. This was indeed the home of a wealthy man.

Meimei had never imagined that her unfortunate life would take such a positive turn. No matter that her husband, Ni Chyan, had but few years to live, that his movements were feeble, that he needed constant care. If she endeared herself to him, she would never feel want again.

Meimei had known much sadness. The youngest of five brothers and sisters, she was but nine years old when her father died. She never forgot how his body, clad in his burial garment, was laid out in their two-room cottage, how her mother had grieved, wringing her hands and beseeching heaven to help her find the money with which to bury her husband.

It was only after a sickening smell began to emanate from the corpse that Meimei's mother came to a desperate decision.

Hand in hand, mother and child walked to the marketplace of the nearest village. There, the mother tied a single straw stalk in Meimei's shiny black hair. Passersby would know she was for sale.

A rough-looking man, unkempt and coarsely clad, began to bargain with her mother. As soon as they reached an agreement, the man grabbed Meimei's arm and tore her from her mother's side. The mother, without once looking back, walked hurriedly away. Feeling utterly abandoned, Meimei began to whimper and then to wail. She was slapped across the face, picked up bodily and hurled into a cart.

For the next six years Meimei served as a slave girl. At the first light of dawn she was up feeding the chickens, cleaning the pig pen, weeding the vegetable garden. She cooked, swept and fetched water from the well. She turned into a drudge, too tired to think, hope or dream, welcoming only the darkness of night when she fell, entirely spent, on the earthen floor.

One night her master came home besotted with wine. Meimei had learned to fear him most after he had been drinking. Then he would turn cruel, force himself upon her, and if she resisted, beat her unmercifully. She heard him approach and shrank beneath her quilt. He leaned over her until the foul odor of his breath assailed her nostrils. Utterly revolted, she shoved him aside, sprang to her feet, and ran out into the dark night. She hoped that in his inebriated state he would not be able to follow.

By sunrise Meimei had arrived at the outskirts of a small city. Midday found her wandering aimlessly through busy streets, her stomach cramped with hunger, her feet sore. A strange woman approached, offering her food and shelter if she would follow her. Responding to the first kind gesture Meimei had received in a long time, she agreed. The woman led her to a house where men sought entertainment in the company of young girls. Here Meimei spent her youthful years learning to become a singsong girl. The older prostitutes taught her many popular tunes, which she sang in a sweet, lilting voice. By the time she reached her late teens, she had become a favorite with the customers. Among the patrons who repeatedly requested the company of the attractive Meimei was Ni Chyan, Shanji's father.

From the beginning Ni Chyan was especially drawn to Meimei, for, unlike the other singsong girls, she respected his advanced years and treated him with deference. She entertained him with her melodies, chatted pleasantly with him over a cup of tea, and when they were alone she gently massaged his old, aching body. In her company, Ni Chyan forgot that his son was a good-for-nothing gambler and that his son's wife had borne no children.

Ni Chyan chose to spend more and more time with Meimei. He showered her with gifts of silks and jewels, and for her favors he always paid generously. The old widower became enchanted with the charming Meimei. He longed for her to be always at his side.

From the day he brought her to his home, Meimei more than fulfilled Ni Chyan's expectations. She catered to his needs and was always ready to please him. whether he wished to stroll in the courtyard or have her prepare his favorite dish of tender, cooked chicken. During the long nights, Ni Chyan no longer tossed and turned, aware of the nearness of death. Sleeping close to Meimei, he felt warm and at peace. Each morning he awoke happy to welcome the new day. His bowed back became straighter, his steps firmer. Blood coursed freely through his veins. He almost felt young again.

The single shadow clouding Ni Chyan's happiness was cast by his only son. From the moment Ni Chyan introduced Shanji to Meimei, there was animosity between them. Dismayed by Shanji's icy stare and grim expression, the pleasant smile on Meimei's face would vanish whenever they were in the same room. Shanji's ill-concealed hatred for Meimei disturbed his elderly father. But Ni Chyan, determined to enjoy every day of life left to him, ignored his son's rude behavior.

Ni Chyan's happiness knew no bounds when Meimei told him that she was with child.

"Meimei, my sweet one," he would murmur, over and over. "You have given me the priceless gift of restored youth. Who would have thought I could father a child at my age?"

Shanji did not fail to notice the gradual rounding of Meimei's slender body. Surprised that his aged father still had the power to sire an offspring gave way to apprehension lest the baby be a male child and thus be entitled to a share of Ni Chyan's wealth.

If he had disliked Meimei before, Shanji now regarded her with intense loathing. "I will not be done out of my fortune because of this singsong girl, this whore, who has twisted my father about her little finger," he vowed again and again.

The day Meimei gave birth to a son Ni Chyan made plans for a great celebration. It was summer, the days long, the evenings warm. He would arrange to have the inner courtyard festooned with lanterns, and he would invite all his friends and relatives. There would be platters of red eggs, boiled chicken, fried pork, roasted duck, whole steamed fish and bean curd with sauteed vegetables. Truly a feast worthy of the occasion! Brimming over with joy, Ni Chyan prepared to greet his guests.

On the morning of the feast, the sun rose in a clear sky. By noon Ni Chyan anxiously awaited the first arrivals. Happiness reigned in the courtyard; that is, for all except one. The more lavish the preparations, the more indignant Shanji became. It was disgusting the way his father was wasting his wealth on a harlot's child! Well, he, for one, would not attend the celebration.

Shanji's wife, however, was of a different mind. "You must

show your face if only for propriety's sake," she insisted. At her urging, Shanji reluctantly consented to make an appearance.

The scene sickened him. There was Meimei, arrayed in an elegant silk gown, and next to her, in a beautiful rocking basket, lay her infant son, Shanwen. Bearing gifts, the guests took turns wishing the baby long life and prosperity. Watching all the merriment only served to heighten Shanji's bitterness. So great was his resentment, dark thoughts entered his mind. He seriously considered killing his half-brother.

Under the loving care of his mother and to the delight of his father, little Shanwen showed signs of developing into a strong, healthy child. After each feeding he would kick his chubby feet and gurgle contentedly. Often his parents would move his sleeping basket into the courtyard. While Shanwen slept peacefully, they chatted and enjoyed the fresh air.

One pleasant summer day, Ni Chyan and Meimei had retired to the courtyard as was their usual practice. Ni Chyan noticed that Meimei seemed out of sorts. She spoke hardly a word and stared pensively into space. This was uncharacteristic for his normally animated wife, and Ni Chyan knew that something was amiss.

"Is something troubling you, my dear?" he asked.

"The truth is that I have been sick with worry for a long time but did not wish to cause you any concern." Meimei was relieved that her husband had presented her with an opportunity to unburden herself.

"I am anxious because of Shanji. He frightens me. On his daily visits he seems courteous, but whenever he glances toward Shanwen's cradle, his eyes narrow and a cruel expression passes over his face. My heart is filled with terror for I fear he may be planning to harm the child."

Trying to assuage her fears, Ni Chyan took Meimei's hand in his own and patted it gently. "Although my body is old, my mind is sharp. Do not fear. I shall not depart this earth until our little one's future is secured."

Before Shanji arrived for his next filial visit, Ni Chyan settled on a plan. After the two exchanged a few polite words, Ni Chyan came right to the point. "You are my eldest son, Shanji, and I give you my sacred word that you alone will be my sole heir. My house, my property, my money will be yours. But Shanwen is also my son and I must consider his welfare. I have been thinking about the old vacant house that stands in the back field. It has been neglected for many years and is of no worth. It is my wish that upon my death you permit Meimei and Shanwen to make their home in that house. Furthermore, when Shanwen reaches manhood I ask that you cede to him enough fertile land so he may earn a modest living. And one more request. You are to give him a small sum of money, enough to permit him to take a wife. Are you agreeable?"

Shanji was elated. He would have everything he wanted in exchange for a promise that required little sacrifice on his part. The old house would be no loss to him, and many years would go by before he would have to part with either cash or acreage. From that moment Shanji banished all thought of doing away with his younger brother.

Meimei's concern, however, was not lessened when Ni Chyan told her of his meeting with Shanji. "My respected husband," she politely countered, "I am only twenty-one, and you are over eighty. One day I shall be alone and at the mercy of Shanji. I do not trust that he will honor his promise after we are parted."

"I have given this matter much thought." Ni Chyan paused and shook his head. "Unfortunately, I, too, harbor doubts that Shanji will be trustworthy. Come with me," he said, leading her into his study. From a cabinet he withdrew a scroll, untied the ribbon around it and unfurled it. Meimei saw a portrait of a staid official seated on a carved chair. Winding up the scroll, Ni Chyan handed it to Meimei. "Hide it where it will be safe from all eyes. After I am gone, should Shanji refuse to hold to the promise he made to me, you are to take the scroll to a wise judge. He will be able to uncover a clue contained in the portrait, a clue that will relieve you of all worries."

Within the year Ni Chyan's life came to an end. Well before the period of mourning was over, Shanji and his wife took up residence in the more desirable east quarters of Ni Chyan's house while Meimei and Shanwen moved into the dilapidated house in the far field.

To make the old place livable, Meimei cleaned the unused *kang* and spread clean quilts over it. She swept the dirt floor, brushed away the cobwebs, and dusted off a shaky table and two low stools, the only pieces of furniture she could find.

Little Shanwen, cheerful and merry, gave purpose to Meimei's quiet life. Her devotion to her son grew with each passing year as did her concern with his future. Whenever worrisome thoughts troubled her she would think of the precious scroll safely hidden behind a loose wallboard. Ni Chyan had not revealed the secret it contained, only that it guaranteed her safety against hard times. Perhaps everything would go well.

The years followed one upon the other until Shanwen reached his eighteenth birthday. Meimei divulged to him his father's final instructions.

"Now you are to visit your elder brother," she told him, "and ask that he fulfill his solemn promise to his father."

After Ni Chyan's death, the two brothers had rarely seen one another. Shanji had stubbornly refused to accept Shanwen as part of the family. He considered him a bastard to be regarded with disdain.

"What are you doing here?" Shanji demanded when his brother came to call on him. He did not try to mask his annoyance.

"I am Shanwen, your brother," the handsome slender young man replied. "May I have the pleasure of speaking with you?"

"My brother!" Shanji snorted. "The son of a whore is no brother to me."

Shanwen was deeply hurt by the insults, yet he persisted.

"Whatever your feelings may be, I am our father's second son. I have come to ask that you honor the agreement you made with him, that you give me what is rightfully mine, a parcel of land and enough money so I may be able to take a wife."

"What an audacious upstart you are," Shanji sputtered. "You are nothing to me. There was no agreement. If you do not leave my presence at once, I shall have you thrown out. What's more, you are old enough to provide for yourself. These many years I have permitted you to live on my land. Instead of appreciation for my kindness, you come to make more demands. Very well, then, neither you nor your shameless mother deserves further charity. Nor will I suffer your presence any longer. Within the month you are to remove yourselves from the house I have so generously made available to you and never set foot on my property again.''

Shanwen realized it was useless to continue the conversation.

"I am not surprised," Meimei told Shanwen when he reported what had happened. "But he shall not have his way."

Early the next morning, with the treasured portrait tucked under her arm, Meimei set out for Kaifeng to register a complaint before the esteemed Lord Bau. Just outside the imposing *yamen* gate, Meimei saw a huge black drum resting in a wooden rack. She picked up the drumstick lying next to it and pounded the drum twice. The reverberating noise brought a guard to the door.

"What do you want?" he questioned.

"I have been wronged," answered Meimei, "and I wish to ask the wise judge for help."

Ushered into a spacious hall, Meimei was directed to kneel until Lord Bau made his entrance.

Meimei was thankful that Lord Bau arrived promptly. Her knees had begun to ache. Her eyes followed the dignified judge clad in his official robe as he lowered himself into his wide armchair. Picking up a heavy wooden mallet, he slammed it hard on the surface of the desk.

"State your complaint," he boomed.

Meimei wished she could flee. The judge's dark countenance frightened her. Could she trust this austere official to trouble himself about the fate of a lowly woman and her child?

"My son has been wrongfully denied his inheritance by his older brother," she began in a quavering voice.

"How did this come about?" Lord Bau's sentences were clipped. He was accustomed to wasting few words.

It was then that Meimei began her woeful tale. She spoke of her unfortunate childhood, her years of enslavement to a cruel master and of her escape to the brothel. She told of Ni Chyan's kindness and the few blissful years she had spent as his wife. She related how the birth of her son had aroused envy in his older brother. Now that her son had reached the age of eighteen, Shanji refused to respect his dead father's wishes and chose to deny his younger brother his rightful share of their father's wealth.

"This my husband gave me before he died," said Meimei, holding out the scroll. "He instructed me to seek out a wise judge capable of unlocking the secret message it contains. I beg Your Honor to examine the scroll closely, for if you can decipher its meaning you will spare my son great hardship."

Lord Bau unrolled the scroll and laid it flat on his desk. A stony-faced official seated in a high-backed chair stared back at him. His left hand resting on his lap was hidden within an ample sleeve. His right hand emerged from the folds of his robe show-ing clearly drawn fingers. It was a pleasing picture, skillfully painted, but Lord Bau could read no message from it, at least at first glance. Stating that he needed more time to examine the portrait, he told Meimei to return home and await further word.

Lord Bau, being an astute judge of character, believed that Meimei had told him the truth. He wanted to help her and was determined to uncover the mysterious message within the scroll. Meticulously he scrutinized every square inch of the portrait. The clue continued to elude him. As if by some strange and powerful force, his eyes were drawn back again and again to the official's right hand. The index finger was slightly separated from the oth-ers and pointed downward.

Lord Bau knew that artists sometimes depicted the human hand in symbolic ways. A finger pointing upwards might mean, "Look toward heaven." A finger pointed inward suggested, "Look to the heart." A finger pointing downward could signify, "Look toward the earth." Following this reasoning, Lord Bau concentrated on the lower end of the scroll.

With little difficulty he removed the small round knobs that

This is the scroll my husband gave me before he died.

held the bottom rod of the scroll. He examined the rod and found nothing unusual. He picked up one of the knobs and turned it over in his hands. Nothing. The other knob produced a surprise. In the hole that had been drilled out to hold one end of the rod, Lord Bau found a tightly rolled piece of paper. He gently pried it loose. Careful not to tear it, he smoothed out the almost transparent slip on which a set of instructions had been written in beautifully styled characters. Lord Bau read:

> Aware of the selfishness of my
> eldest son, Shanji, I do not
> expect that he will honor the
> agreement we made prior to my death.
> Should he fail to cede to his
> brother the parcel of land and the
> sum of money stipulated in the
> agreement, I have provided for my
> youngest son to inherit a goodly
> sum. Buried beneath Meimei's
> house, near the east wall, are
> five thousand pieces of silver.
> An equal amount will be found on the
> west side, together with a lacquered box
> containing ten ounces of gold. The
> silver is my bequest to my second
> son, Shanwen. The gold is a reward
> for the wise judge who unravels the
> riddle of the scroll.

Lord Bau smiled. His hunch had paid off. The finger pointing downward had indeed proven to be the important clue.

Lord Bau summoned a messenger. "You are to arrange for Shanji, Meimei and Shanwen to gather together in the main hall of Shanji's house after the last light fades from the sky. They are to wait there for my arrival."

Lord Bau and two of his aides reached Shanji's home after dark. Shanji, Meimei and Shanwen were all present. Shanji wore a long face. He felt ill at ease for he could think of no reason why the most highly respected and honored judge would wish to visit him and why he had insisted that Meimei and Shanwen be present, too.

Lord Bau ordered all lamps extinguished.

"No doubt you are wondering why you have been asked to assemble here in the darkness of night." The judge's resonant voice commanded everyone's rapt attention. "I shall explain. The spirit of Ni Chyan appeared to me as I slept. He asked that I come here to meet with you. He cannot rest peacefully in his grave until an important family problem is resolved. I have come to do his bidding."

A single moonbeam penetrated the inky blackness of the room, casting strangely shaped shadows on the wall. No one stirred. Time seemed to stand still, and for long minutes nothing transpired. Then, without warning, Lord Bau's voice shattered the silence.

"Yes, I hear you, Ni Chyan, but your words are very faint. What is it that you are saying?" Lord Bau cocked his head as though he were straining to hear. "You say that when Shanwen was a baby your elder son, Shanji, threatened to harm him, perhaps murder him? Yes, yes, please go on, your voice is clearer now. Shanji was afraid he would have to divide his inheritance with his brother? He wanted it all for himself? Yes I understand. In return for your assurance that he would be your sole benefactor, Shanji agreed that when the time came he would give Shanwen some land and enough money to take a wife? You say Shanji failed to honor his word?"

Again, Lord Bau seemed to be finding it difficult to hear. "Ni Chyan, are you there? Is there more you wish to tell?" Lord Bau waited. Finally, he said, "I believe Ni Chyan has left us. He speaks no more. Please turn up the lights."

Astounded by Lord Bau's power to contact those beyond the grave, Shanji, Meimei and Shanwen regarded him with wonderment.

Now Lord Bau focused his attention on Shanji. He did not hide his displeasure.

"What have you to say on your own behalf?" he demanded.

Guilt-ridden and fearing what might happen next, Shanji sought to appease Lord Bau.

"I will give him the land, I will give him the money," he blurted out.

"So shall it be," agreed Lord Bau. "You will also give him the house in which he and his mother have lived, all that is in it, all that is beneath it, all that is to either side of it."

"Whatever you ask, Master."

Shanji's willing compliance was not due to a sincere change of heart. What he had offered to grant required no sacrifice on his part. The old house, the land around it, were of little worth. He was delighted to be let off so easily.

"Please leave us." Lord Bau waved his arm, dismissing Shanji. From his waistband he withdrew the small note he had found in the knob of the scroll. He read it aloud for Meimei and Shanwen.

"Ni Chyan has fulfilled his obligation to his family," said Lord Bau. "He was a good man whose name is to be honored."

Meimei and Shanwen, accompanied by Lord Bau and his aides, walked to Meimei's small dwelling. Though it was still hours before dawn, the aides set about digging a trench along the east wall inside the house. The hardpacked earthen floor did not yield easily to their picks. It was a slow, laborious task. Shanwen helped by holding aloft two lanterns.

Shanji had retired for the night, but his troubled thoughts kept him awake. He rose from his bed and stood at the window, trying to fight off the dejection Lord Bau's visit had caused. Wrapped up in his own thoughts, he did not at first notice the light shining in Meimei's house. Bitten with curiosity, he dressed and went to investigate.

"What are you doing?" he asked of Lord Bau's aides.

"Looking for a treasure," one of them replied. Shanji did not take the answer seriously. He was about to repeat the question when the aide's shovel struck a hard object. Everyone's attention was riveted on him while he dug out the first earthen jar. Encouraged by the discovery, the aide dug with more vigor. Soon, four similar jars were unearthed. Shanji was dumbfounded.

Each time another jar was brought to light,
there was a murmur of surprise.

"Move to the other side of the house," Lord Bau directed. The digging continued under the watchful gaze of everyone present. Each time another jar was brought to light there was a murmur of surprise. A small, lacquered box was the last thing to be lifted out. The lids of the jars were pried open. In the glare of Shanwen's lanterns hundreds of pieces of silver shone like the stars, and in the lacquered box lay ten ounces of brilliant gold.

Unable to contain his anger, Shanji stamped his foot, turned his back on the jubilant group and left, mumbling incoherently. His father's heavy hand had reached out from the grave against him.

In profound gratitude for his help, Meimei offered Lord Bau the box of gold. Lord Bau shook his head. His lips parted in a smile.

"No, no, I do not wish to accept any reward. Only remember to use your new wealth wisely. Happy are those blessed with the gift of riches. Happier still are those who share their bounteous gift with others."

YIN-LIEN CHIN teachers Chinese at Vassar College. YETTA CENTER and MILDRED ROSS are both writers and retired teachers. The three co-authored *Dragons in a Flowery Land: An Introduction to Chinese History and Culture* (1985), and *Traditional Chinese Folktales* (1989). All are residents of New York State's Hudson Valley. LU WANG is an artist whose work has been widely published. He is an editor of *The Teacher* magazine in Shaanxi, China.